BREAKING THROUGH

Developing Healthy Relationships

by Clive E. Neil

Bogota, New Jersey

TABLE OF CONTENTS

Foreword   *i*

Preface   *v*

Introduction : Understanding Community   1

Chapter I   The Concept of Marriage in the African American Culture   15

Chapter II   Marriage - Sharing in the Image of God   33

Chapter III   Biblical Understanding of Marriage   53

Chapter IV   Methods of Handling Conflict   67

Chapter V   Learning to Love Again   85

Chapter VI   The Design and Implementation of the Marriage
              Enrichment Program   95

Chapter VII   A Plan for Action   109

Appendix A   125
Appendix B   126
Appendix C   127
Orientation Session (Appendix D)   132
Appendix E   136
Appendix F   139

BREAKING THROUGH
Developing Healthy Relationships

ISBN 1-889389-06-4

Unless otherwise indicated, all Scripture quotations are from the King James Version of the Bible.

Typesetter: Carolyn Davis

FOREWORD

Dr. Clive Neil's call to the Bedford Central Presbyterian Church, located in northern Brooklyn, thrust him into a community besieged by a myriad of socio-economic problems with no or few solutions in sight. In a community where drugs are sold openly and poverty is experienced by over fifty percent of the residents, dysfunctional, unstable family arrangements are quite prevalent. The demanding needs for the survival of single parents as well as the nuclear-type family, both in and out of the church, became one of Rev. Neil's pressing long-range goals.

Early in his ministry at Bedford Central Presbyterian Church, marital counseling consumed an inordinate amount of his pastoral time. It became apparent to him that the church was not equipping couples to manage conflict and stress effectively. It is commonly said that the first year of marriage is extremely crucial. In my estimation, after twenty-four years of marriage, not only is every year, but every day is crucial with the likelihood of some degree of conflict developing out of the blue over some insignificant incident.

The overall goal of this enlightening book is to provide couples married within five years with the needed insights and skills that will enable them to deal more effectively with marital conflict. Basically, Dr. Neil's intent is to help families stay together with the realization that ". . . many marriages would benefit greatly if the husband and wife only knew that conflict in marriage is inevitable, that conflict belongs indeed to the essence of marriage." (Plattner, P.)

In this delightfully written book, Dr. Neil clearly points out the sociological, psychological, biblical and theological concept "that it is not conflict per se that is so destructive to the marriage relationship, but it is the failure to resolve or to utilize conflict appropriately" (Bach & Wyden). He covers such dynamic topics as: marriage in the Bible, models for mutual relationships, the matter of anger, methods of handling conflict, and a formula for growth in conflict. He also aptly depicts the concept of marriage in the African-American family from its West African roots to the demise and demonic treatment of the black family during slavery.

It was his ardent desire to design a practical marriage enrichment model which would help couples understand the depth and importance of **mutuality** or **mutual submissiveness** in the first institution created by God. Dr. Neil's exegesis of (shedding light on) Genesis 2:24 and Ephesians 5:31, two individuals "becoming one flesh" will cause you to reexamine these passages and see them in the light of God's original creation of maleness and femaleness as it relates to the *Imago Dei*. Dr. Neil demystifies this unique model of mutual relationship in marriage as presented in Ephesians 5:21-33, which proclaims, "be subject one to another out of reverence for Christ." This passage significantly lifts up mutuality in relationships.

Through the pastoral voice of Dr. Neil, the church is challenged to be serious and intentional about equipping married couples with the tools to deal with conflict in marriage. In this book, you will be motivated to rethink the vows taken and strive to carry out the mandates of the Creator to ". . . leave . . ., " ". . . cleave . . ." and ". . . become one . . ."

One significant benefit from this marriage enrichment program developed by Dr. Neil is to see that marriages remain intact, healthy, Christ-centered, and endure "until death do us part." The ultimate benefit is that with sound, stable marriages capable of dealing with conflict, we will produce strong functional families. It is a universal axiom that strong families are the building blocks of a strong nation.

I consider Dr. Neil's volume to be a milestone contribution to marriages in conflict, the family and the church in general.

With great joy, I present to you **Breaking Through**, by Rev. Dr. Clive E. Neil.

Rev. Edward Davis, B.A., M.Div.
Pastor
Presbyterian Church of St. Albans

PREFACE

When two people find themselves together for a lifetime — both with an abundance of thoughts, feelings, opinions, and interests — they have a chance to build a magnificent marriage. Blending the uniqueness of one partner with the uniqueness of the other takes great skill, but the potential for a totally new corporate identity with maximum breadth and depth is an incredibly valuable goal to pursue.

To have a great marriage, there must be two authentic partners. Authenticity involves the full and free expression of each person's true self, with all of its uniqueness. When both persons are fully authentic, their complete agreement on everything is highly unlikely.

A relationship doesn't need both of its partners if they are exactly the same. The wonderful thing you do for your partner is to share that part of you that is different from your mate. But, as sure as you share your differences there is bound to be conflict. This conflict is healthy and gives the opportunity to expand your marriage.

Therein lies a marriage-building strategy designed to expand the boundaries of your corporate lives and to increase the range of your relationship. Imagine a marriage in which one person wants everything about their lives together to be precisely the same. This simply wouldn't be much of a marriage; it would merely be two people living one life. For the person whose uniqueness was ignored and never incorporated, there would inevitably be a sense of not counting much, an intense feeling that his or her ideas, tastes, and preferences were unimportant, unnecessary and unwanted.

Conversely, a marriage in which each person brings ideas, attitudes, and approaches — even to the point of creating disagreements — is a marriage that will build on the best that both partners have to offer.

The bottom line in this book is this: conflict that is mismanaged can destroy a marriage. It can turn the whole relationship into a battleground where the only winners are sure to be eventual losers — and the losers are sure to be filled with resentment. If the couple decides to eliminate all conflict in the name of maintaining peace, there will be a terrible price to pay. The individuals' uniqueness is likely to become more and more repressed and stifled. They will have to develop a mask to hide their frustrations. This kind of relationship is bound to become cold and distant.

Most of us know couples who are constantly fighting like cats and dogs, but they sincerely love each other. Indeed they have a very healthy marriage, though you may find this surprising.

What my research and practice have taught me is the amount of conflict in a marriage only determines the speed at which the marriage is moving toward greatness or toward destruction. People, if they desire, can sit still in their marriages, rule out conflict, but that marriage will eventually crash. Instead, one needs to learn the skills necessary for managing conflict. Well-managed conflict is like a stairway that can lead to higher and higher levels of marital greatness.

I get anxious when persons come to me for premarital counseling and say they have never had a single argument. They are strangers to a crucial part of married life. They lack the slightest idea about their combined skillfulness to handle that part of marriage that brings so much potential for positive or negative change. If any couple thinks they are not going to have disagreements, they are tragically self-deceived and headed for trouble. According to the statistics, fifty percent of all divorces takes place within three years of the wedding day. Think of that fact! Couples get married, encounter conflict, give up — all within three years.

There are two points to be considered. First, these couples must have been profoundly unaware of how challenging it is to make a marriage work, and they were certainly unaware of the number of conflicts that would arise. Second, they must have been alarmingly ill-equipped to handle their conflicts. The management of conflict is a complex but entirely learnable skill. Unfortunately, these couples never developed this skill, at least not to the required level of proficiency.

Conflict is a necessary part of every marriage for as long as marriage lasts. If there is no conflict, or if conflict suddenly slows down or levels off, it is a sign that something is wrong with the marriage. There are countless reasons for no conflict, but they all indicate a reduction in that part of a marriage that gives it the potential for growth and change. The good news is that even the most entrenched conflict avoiders can improve. In fact, even those who are pretty good at conflict resolution.

This book attempts to analyze the development of a marriage relationship through a biblical and psychological perspective. To effectively accomplish this task, a historical approach was necessary to point out some of the resources and constraints that present day relationships will encounter. The biblical examination was crucial to fully understand both the starting point and the ending basis of human relationship.

Appreciation and thanks are due to a number of people who were instrumental in the completion of this thesis project. It was the contribution of many dedicated individuals who gave of their time and encouraging words which motivated me.

My sincere gratitude goes out to the Law Advisory Committee and all the Project workers. It was the interest, constructive criticism and patience of my advisor, Dr. Paul Smith that prodded me to the end. Dr. Heather Elkins, my project reader offered many constructive suggestions.

The person who provided unflagging support through the good as well as difficult times was my wife Faye. Through the sleepless hours she assured Aisha and Darius that Daddy would come home soon. I could not have made it without them. Agnes Alexander faithfully typed and retyped the manuscript. Patricia Gordon used her expertise to edit the manuscript. Special thanks to Cecilia Channell-Cherry for her editorial and typing assistance. As participants in the Marriage Enrichment Program, the six couples who shared the experience contributed immensely. So it is to all of those persons that I express my gratitude. Finally, to the officers and members of Bedford Central Presbyterian Church for their openness to change and creative ministry.

INTRODUCTION

UNDERSTANDING COMMUNITY

WHAT DO WE MEAN BY COMMUNITY?

Webster's New World Dictionary defines the word "COMMUNITY" derived from the Latin word "communitas," which means fellowship. The word "COMMUNITY" means all the people living in a particular district, city or as a smaller social unit within a larger one, having similar interests, work, etc. In common with Webster's definition is Doob in *Sociology: An Introduction.* His definition is that a community "is a settlement of people living in a specific geographical area and maintaining a system of interrelationship that satisfies many of the people's physical and social needs."[1] Because of the interrelationships among its inhabitants, a community is normally a source of group identifications.

A community should be considered in terms of the sources of residential satisfaction, relationships between people of varying cultures and background, and their sense of closeness to other community members. It is felt that during times of personal and family crisis such as birth, death, illness, fire or catastrophe, most communities would typically display their neighborliness. Therefore, the community should not be defined of only as an area with residential buildings, churches, schools, the corner shops, and trees lined neatly in rows by the roadside, but instead as the

---

[1]Christopher Doobs, *"Sociology: An Introduction,"* (New York: Holt, Rinehart Inc., 1988) p. 86.

individuals living and working in those buildings. Their social ranking, largely based on occupational roles, encompasses power, income, wealth, family prestige, education, lifestyle, and material possessions. There are also some of the criteria used within the community for evaluating individuals.

The Bedford Central Presbyterian Church community is located in Northern Brooklyn and consists of four neighborhoods: Prospect Heights, Weeksville, Brower Park and Crown Heights. The name Brooklyn itself, derives from the Dutch word "Breukelen" which meant "broken valley" and was originally six villages. Bedford Central is bound on the north by Atlantic Avenue, on the east by Ralph Avenue, on the south by Eastern Parkway, and on the west by Flatbush Avenue. The neighborhood in which I work and will focus on is Crown Heights, sandwiched among Park Slope and Bedford Stuyvesant, Brownsville, East Flatbush, and Prospect Park.

Crown Heights was a quiet, sparsely populated settlement in the original Dutch town of Breukelen (Brooklyn) first known as Crow Hill. Crown Heights actually included a succession of hills in the early 1900's, and for reasons unknown Crow permanently picked up its "n." The Carcarsee Indians, the original inhabitants of Brooklyn, lived on what is now New York Bay and spoke Algonkian. The Dutch established their first settlement in 1624. When the City of New York established its system of community planning districts in 1968, a major community development agency in Bedford Stuyvesant considered the neighborhood to be substantially larger, and included areas of Atlantic Avenue South to Eastern Parkway, designating it as Crown Heights for purposes of city planning.

3

In 1920, Crown Heights was predominantly a white neighborhood. By the 1970's the identifiable subcommunities included Hispanics in the northeastern area, middle-class blacks in the central brownstone section, and a large number of recent immigrants from the islands of the Caribbean who settled primarily in the southern area near Eastern Parkway. More recently, the area south of Atlantic Avenue has been considered a part of Crown Heights. Due to the pattern of rigid housing segregation, a kind of tri-ethnic school system developed with the northern tier of the borough, being a predominantly Hispanic school system, while Fort Green to Crown Heights was an overwhelmingly black system. In the 1960's due to high levels of unemployment among the black youth, an appeal was made to Mayor Robert Wagner. In 1965 Youth in Action became the officially sanctioned local community action program with agencies established in Crown Heights. The population in 1988 consisted of approximately one million and continued to increase at an average annual rate of 6%. The birth rate in 1987 was 22.5 per 1000 of the population while the death rate was 9.1 per 1000 of the population. The Bedford Central Presbyterian Church was founded in 1894 when there was a growing awareness of the need for a spiritual awakening in the American society in general, and in Brooklyn in particular. As history of the Church written in 1989 states:

> The Classes of Brooklyn have cause to mourn over the prevalence of vice and immorality within their bounds. Our contiguity to the Cities of New York and Brooklyn exposes us to witness a great profanation of the Sabbath.

On close examination, we observe that Brooklyn was experiencing some of the major problems prevalent in those times. Handy, in his book, *A Christian America*, informs us that it was an era when crusades were formed to combat the vices of the profanation of the Sabbath and drinking. There was revivalism in many forms against these powerful forces and there was emphasis on personal morality. The church was greatly concerned about gambling, dancing, smoking.[1]

Over the past 150 years, there has been a change of attitude in the local community as well as in society at large. Some of the issues of the last century have become today's non-issues. The church, which in the nineteenth century fought for Sabbath observance, is today a part of a community which accepts such Sunday activities as major league sports, marches and picnics in the parks, to name just a few. Many churches promote dancing for fellowship and fund raising. Alcoholic beverages are raffled in many church halls. It is ironic that churches which accommodate Alcoholic Anonymous groups will tacitly promote the use of alcohol.

One other change in the local congregation of Bedford Central has been in the racial composition of its members. Initially, the church ministered exclusively to a white community. With the construction of low-income housing referred to as "The Projects" in 1947, the composition of the community gradually changed. As the black and Hispanic populations increased, the white population decreased and this was reflected in the membership of the church. Today, ninety-seven percent of the membership is black. The project comprises 1100 families in 22 buildings. Of this, over fifty percent are single parents, and over sixty percent receive some form of public assistance. In other words, at least one of every two homes receives welfare or is a single-parent household. It is logical

---

[1]Robert Handy, "*A Christian America,*" (New York: Oxford United Press, 1984) p. 143.

5

to assume that many of these homes have both problems. These figures are staggering when compared with reports that in the state of New York only thirteen percent of white children live in poor households. The Bedford community is plagued by a variety of problems with few solutions in sight. The Central Bureau Census of 1987 indicates that whereas the proportion of white Americans living in poverty declined significantly in recent years, the proportion of black and Hispanic Americans has increased steadily.[1]

Poverty is caused by unemployment and under-employment. One of the consequences is hunger and another is crime. Both hunger and crime are prevalent in Brooklyn. Drugs are sold openly and muggings are frequent. Homicide is not unusual. In my five years as a minister, I have performed funeral rites for three murdered young men, one for an AIDS victim as the result of intravenous drug use, and two for young men, the result of drug overdoses. My ministry includes visiting both young men and women who are incarcerated, as well as providing support for their families. Added to the above is the problem of education. In a community where drugs are sold openly and poverty is experienced by over fifty percent of the residents, it seems hardly surprising that there is little motivation for young people to stay in school. The staggering statistic that fifty-four percent of black high school students in New York State fail to graduate is clearly reflected in Brooklyn. A major contributing factor to the dropout rate is the prevalence of teenage pregnancy.

---

[1]Martin Tolchin, "Minority Poverty on Rise but White Poor Decline," *(New York Times*, January 1, 1988).

An area of challenge in my ministry is addressing the care of senior citizens. There is a need for adequate health care. Some senior citizens are in need of companionship, while others live in overcrowded conditions brought about by the inability of their own offspring, who are single parents, to provide accommodation for themselves and their children. In a situation such as this, it is not surprising that some seniors and their offspring experience hunger. Some of the families, in trying to solve the problems of overcrowding and hunger, have resorted to ejecting young families, who in turn have had to seek refuge in public shelters. Brooklyn has its share of homeless families.

Another problem I have to face is ministering to members of the church family who have been the victims of crime perpetrated against them by other members of the church family. This stifles growth and fellowship within the church and requires sensitivity, strong leadership and resourcefulness. As I read Richard Shaull's *Heralds of a New Reformation*, in which he describes the poor of Latin America, I am reminded of our church in Brooklyn when he says:

The church of Jesus Christ is made up of those who are rejected, despised and abandoned; those who are considered useless, incapable of doing anything and have believed what society says about them.[1]

In addition to those sociological problems mentioned in Brooklyn there is a spiritual inertia among the people. The church emphasizes a liturgy to causes created in the sixteenth century to

---

[1]Richard Shaull, *Heralds of a New Reformation* (New York: Maryknoll, 1984), p. 121.

7

meet the needs of the environment, thus there is a constant struggle to break loose from the cold formalism of the past. Today, we are in the process of changing our pattern of worship so as to better reflect the culture of the community and membership. Another major aspect of the spiritual inertia in the church is manifested through the stewardship of the membership. Poverty, a factor previously alluded to, plays a deciding role in attitudes and patterns of stewardship.

Not all families in the church of Bedford Central are numbered among the poor. There are some professional and progressive families who have chosen to remain in the community. The observation made by Steimle, Niedenthal and Rice in their book, *Preaching the Story*, is applicable. They state that there is need for "a Gospel for the well, the effective, the joyous, the busy, engaged people of this world."[1] In the diversity of experiences at Bedford, there is recognition of the commonality of our human experiences and the uniqueness of the Gospel Story to respond to them. These experiences are all within the parameter of the 'Kerygma' — the Good News, which is revealed in the person of Jesus Christ. As pastor, I am called upon like Ezekiel to be amongst my people and to sit where they sit. The challenge of Jesus recorded in Luke 4:18 is ever before me — "The Spirit of the Lord is upon me because He hath anointed me to preach the Gospel to the poor. He hath sent me to heal the broken-hearted, to preach deliverance to the captive, and recovering of sight to the blind; to set at liberty them that are bruised."

---

[1]Steimle, Niedenthal and Rice, *Preaching the Story*, (Philadelphia: Fortress Press, 1980), p. 79.

The challenge of my ministry is to face the myriad of problems in this complex and pluralistic society. I must initiate programs to meet the needs of the affected groups within the church and the community at large. My first commitment must be to help the young people in the community. I need to provide them with spiritual and moral convictions as they face the attraction of drugs, the ease of becoming dropouts, the desecration of their bodies through drunkenness and drug addiction. I need them to further their educational skills so that they can become employable in the society.

My second commitment must be to initiate programs to meet the needs of the adults. I have to seek resources to help those who are hungry and needy. I must provide counseling to those who are bereaved and burdened. I must provide a support system for those whose families are involved in crime and whose children have dashed their highest hopes to pieces. Every Sunday becomes a time of caring, counseling, and challenging my congregation while my personal role becomes one of an enabler.

Marriage offers the promise of being the most meaningful of all human relationships, but the very nature of marriage involves conflict. The reality as well as the inevitability of conflict in marriage is stressed by the Swiss psychiatrist, Paul Plattner. He states that "many marriages would benefit greatly if the husband and wife only knew that conflict in marriage is inevitable, that it belongs indeed to the essence of marriage."[1] However, it is not conflict per se that is so destructive to the marriage relationship. It is often the failure to resolve or utilize conflict appropriately.

---

[1] Paul Plattner, *Conflict and Understanding in Marriage*, trans. John R. Bodo (Richmond, Virginia: John Knox Press, 1970), p. 13.

According to George Bach, a noted therapist, "the inability to manage personal conflicts is at the root of the crisis that threatens the structure of the American family."[1] He goes on to say that "it is inept conflict management rather than inept sex that causes most marriage troubles."[2] William Barry concurs that "the modes of conflict resolution are crucial for the success of the interpersonal situation that is marriage since one can assume that interpersonal conflict is inevitable in any marriage . . ."[3]

Yet very little is being done to equip married couples to manage conflict more effectively. One difficulty in this area as indicated by Judith Laws is that "the literature is sadly lacking in data on conflict management as an aspect of marriage."[4] Thus there needs to be more research undertaken and more resource material written specifically on how to cope more constructively with marital conflict. Another difficulty as noted by Gurman and Rice is that "although most, if not all, marital counselors are concerned with the resolution of conflict in marriage, only a few of these professionals present specific techniques for the

---

[1]George R. Bach and Peter Wyden, *The Intimate Enemy: How to Fight Fair in Love and Marriage*, (New York: William Morrow and Company, Inc. 1969), p. 17.

[2]Ibid., p.128.

[3]William A. Barry, *Marriage Research and Conflict: An Integrative Review*, Psychological Bulletin 73, (January 1970), p. 42.

[4]Judith Long Laws, "A Feminist View of Marital Adjustment", in *Couples in Conflict,* eds. Alan S. Gurman and David D. Rice (New York: Jason Aronson, 1975), p.108.

accomplishment of this goal."[1] Therefore, it is important that the more beneficial techniques and procedures for dealing with conflict between spouses be adequately presented and be made more accessible to couples in general. Still, another difficulty as mentioned by David Mace is that existing data on matters such as conflict management are not being made "dynamically" available to couples to any great extent."[2] Therefore, suitable programs and experiences must be developed and conducted that will permit couples the opportunity to learn dynamically, not just factually, the necessary skills and insights to resolve their conflicts.

From a religious perspective, a further difficulty develops with the incorporation of modern behavioral concepts such as conflict management into one's personal experience of faith. For some Christians, unfortunately, their understanding of biblical teaching precludes the use of such scientific theories and techniques. In a church marriage retreat which I conducted, this very conviction was expressed. One of the participants on an evaluation form stated quite succinctly that "the Bible is our guide for solving the problems of life, not people's ideas about human behavior or social interaction."[3] But the fact of the matter is that the truth of the Bible and the principles of human behavior are not mutually exclusive, but are compatible and complementary. As Samuel

---

[1]Alan S. Gurman and David G. Rice, eds., *Couples in Conflict* (New York: Jason Aronson, 1975), p. 13.

[2]David R. Mace, "We Call It ACME," *Marriage and Family Enrichment: New Perspective and Programs*, ed. Herbert A. Otto (Nashville: Avingdon, 1976), p. 171.

[3]An evaluation statement form of a member at a Marriage Enrichment Retreat conducted at the Tuscarora Inn, Pocono, Pa., February 10-12, 1988.

Southard has remarked, "if only we can bring these two viewpoints together."[1] Hence, it is essential to correlate behavioral concepts with biblical concepts on matters such as marriage and conflict.

In my pastorate, I have been confronted with one other difficulty: the apparent failure of the church in equipping couples to manage conflict more effectively. Since many marriages are solemnized by a religious ceremony, it would seem that the church ought to bear a primary responsibility for undertaking a marriage enrichment program. Married couples in conflict have steadily increased for this pastor as it has for many other ministries. Yet, it is indeed regrettable that the many insights and skills for handling conflict in a constructive manner are seldom made available to these couples until they are in serious trouble. Surely preventative measures are better than remedial ones. In an effort to reverse these trends, it is imperative then for the church to deal with the matter of interpersonal conflict from the very outset of marriage and not just at the terminal point of no return: separation or divorce.

The main objective of this thesis-project is to develop a marriage enrichment program for recently married couples. The actual program is to be structured as a dynamic learning experience rather than a static one. It will be primarily for healthy couples within their first five years of marriage, which is considered to be the formative period.[2] The emphasis will be placed on the human

---

[1] Samuel Southard, *Anger in Love* (Philadelphia: Westminster Press, 1973), p. 9.

[2] Howard J. Clinebell, Jr., *Growth Counseling for Marriage Enrichment* (Philadelphia: Fortress Press, 1975), p. 56.

potential for growth instead of pathological analysis. The overall goal is to provide couples with the needed insights and skills that will enable them to deal more effectively with marital conflict. A review of the doctoral dissertations over the last twenty years reveals that no other doctoral study in either the area of conflict or marriage has reported the completion of the exact same project.[1] Therefore, the development of a marriage enrichment program for recently married couples should be a significant contribution to this field of study.

There are several sub-objectives as well. One sub-objective is to determine, in particular, the important biblical concepts on marriage and conflict. In some cases this will involve a general survey of several key topics in both the Old and New Testaments, while in other cases it will require a detailed exegesis of certain specific passages on the subject in question. Another sub-objective is to present the necessary insights and skills to handle conflict in a positive rather than a negative manner. These theories and techniques are to be drawn from the corresponding fields in the behavioral sciences. A further sub-objective is to demonstrate by way of a brief summary comparison that behavioral science and theology can form a unified conceptual framework for the management of marital conflict. The final sub-objective is to measure the effectiveness of the program developed. A program evaluation form is to be completed by all the participants as an overall assessment of the total program.

---

[1]Dissertation Abstracts International: A — Humanities and Social Sciences, vols. 40.49 (Ann Arbor, Mich: University Microfilms International, 1969 - 79 - 89)

CHAPTER I

THE CONCEPT OF MARRIAGE

IN THE

AFRICAN AMERICAN CULTURE

WHAT IS THE BLACK FAMILY?

The community of Bedford Central is 100% black, with a very strong African orientation toward life. With this fact in mind, one has to consider marriage within the framework of African family structure.

It first must be stated that family stability is a trademark of the Western African societies where most of the forebears of America's black population originated. However, the family structures of Western Africa were not always of the Western European conjugal model. This model did exist, but the primary family model of Western Africa was the consanguineal (blood-related) model.

"African families, like those in other parts of the world, embody two contrasting bases of membership: Consanguinity, which refers to kinship that is commonly assumed or presumed to be biologically based and rooted in blood ties, and affinity which refers to kinship created by law and rooted in law." Conjugality refers specifically to the affinal kinship created between spouses.[1]

---

[1]Niara Suderkasa, "Interpreting the Afro-American Heritage in the Afro-American Family Organization," p. 40 in *Black Families*, edited by Harriet McAdoo. Copyright 1981 by Sage Publications, Inc. Reprinted by permission of Sage Publications, Inc.

The African family structure, unlike the European family structure, tends to form around consanguineal cores of adult siblings. The groups that formed around these core members "included their spouses and children."[1] When African people were married, they "tended not to go off and form new nuclear groupings but instead joined an already existing compound of adjoining or contiguous dwellings,"[2] composed of the extended family members.

In addition to the consanguineal structure in most African societies, there also existed a conjugal structure which was quite different from the European model and often polygynous in makeup. "A number of Western scholars have chosen to characterize the polygynous conjugal family as several district nuclear families with one husband/father in common."[3]

It must be stressed, however, that in the African family system, it was the consanguineal rather than the conjugal model that was paramount. The consanguineal structure was the central factor, in such critical family realities as decision making, settling internal disputes, and the inheritance of land titles, among others. These matters were settled not on the basis of spouse relationship but upon the blood ties of the family compound.

The structure then existed so that the eldest male was most often the head of the family compound. Along with the elders of

---

[1] Ibid., p. 41.

[2] Ibid., p. 41.

[3] Ibid., p. 41.

the group, he was responsible for settling all internal (including conjugal) disputes. Decisions were made separately rather than jointly and husbands and wives often had very distinct responsibilities within the group.

"Excepting those areas where Islamic traditions overshadowed indigenous African traditions, women have a good deal of control over the fruits of their own labor."[1] An interesting result of this was that in spite of the rigidly paternalistic nature of the society, husbands had little control over their wives' properties. In fact, wives in these groupings had considerably more power and influence than did their European sisters.

The socialization of the young was a responsibility of the entire compound. Although the conjugal family had special duties, it was the consanguineal family which ultimately gave the child a sense of identity and self.

The stability of the family was not dependent upon the success of the individual conjugal units. In fact, divorce and remarriage were rather easily accepted in the larger extended structure. Spouses were selected as lifetime compassionate and passionate lovers, but it was never expected that an individual was to be the one totally responsible for the spouse's every need for a lifetime. The African family system was characterized by "respect, restraint, responsibility, and reciprocity."[2]

---

[1]Ibid., p. 32.

[2]Ibid., p. 44.

What one realizes in examining the African extended family structure is that the place of women was certainly much different from the Western world where polygynous structures were viewed as totally demeaning to women. The African structure was built on a mutual respect of women, men, and children. The uniqueness of this system can be seen in the way illegitimacy was handled. Women who had clandestine relationships with men other than their spouses reared offspring of these unions with the same care and love as children of the conjugal unit. The extended system prevented strongly violent reactions to such occurrences. Persons in the extended systems were spared the jealousies which a purely nuclear structure fosters because partners did not see themselves as totally belonging to each other. All persons in this system belonged to the compound, not to any one individual.

Historically, one example of the African family system was found in the Ashanti. Their family system displayed a marvelous balance of respect, restraint, responsibility, and reciprocity. Fathers were responsible for the obedience and moral deference of their children, but with the strictness came tenderness also. An Ashanti proverb reads, "A man has no hold over his children, except through their love." Mothers were given reverential treatment but they also functioned in very practical ways. Unlike our Western Freudian hang-ups, an Ashanti mother was to be her son's best friend. She was the chief counsel in all matters, be they practical, emotional, or physical. The Ashanti mother also was responsible for seeing that her daughters grew up in daily and unbroken intimacy with her. The daughters learned from the mother all the feminine traits of character.

SLAVERY AND THE BLACK FAMILY

Whatever the relative strength or weakness of the African family structure, it must be remembered that African peoples were also forced to face the holocaust of slavery. Slavery systematically attempted to destroy the black family. The insidiousness of its evil cannot be minimized.

Throughout the sunless experience of slavery, families were yanked from the motherland and brought as strangers to an alien place. As C. Eric Lincoln poetically stated, "Slavery was a man getting up for a breath of fresh air and winding up on a boat destined for a new world."[1]

Once Africans arrived in the New World, every attempt was made to strip them of name, dignity, and culture. Even more tragic, morals were forcibly stripped away as well. Black males were encouraged to be irresponsible breeders who served nothing more than two functions — mating and manual labor. Black females were accosted by masters who forced them to have sex and bear unwanted children. To make this systematic rape of black women even worse, laws were changed so that the inheritance for all mulatto children would be traced through the woman's lineage, cutting these children off from access to the master's capital.

Because of the way racism enforced its power through economics, sex amongst the slaves was viewed by the master as a matter of dollars and cents. The encouraging of casual breeding amongst slaves and the wanton rape of slave women were the

---

[1]C. Eric Lincoln: *Before the Mayflower: A History of the Negro in America.* (Chicago: Johnson Publishing Company, 1964), pp. 30-31.

fastest ways to increase the birth rate and improve capital gain. In the words of Robert C. Williamson, "It is difficult to overestimate the dismal effects of slavery on family life."[1] He further states, "Because of the slave owner's encouragement of high birth rate as a means of increasing wealth, little consideration was given to the establishment of a firm marriage bond. Occasionally, the offspring of mixed liaisons were given freedom. It is estimated that one-third of the half million free Negroes in 1860 were mulattos."[2] It can never be stressed enough that the huge mulatto population in America is the result of the rape of black women by white masters.

Slavery enforced the equality of black males and females through equal pain. The master never treated the slave women with any of the daintiness with which he treated white women. Slave women were forced to work in the field side by side with males. They were punished with equal severity and the physical realities of pregnancy or pre-or postnatal care were never considered as reasons for time out from work.

After emancipation, the situation for the family did not improve. The ineffectiveness of the Freedman's Bureau insured that the problems begun during slavery would never adequately be dealt with. Again, economics exacerbated the problem.

The demise of the agrarian life in the South struck a particularly vicious blow to black males who were trained only in farming. Work was scarce to nonexistent. What little work was

---

[1]Robert C. Williamson, *Marriage & Family Relation* (New York: John Wiley & Sons, 1972), p. 81.

[2]Ibid., p.82.

available was the demeaning and menial labor reserved for maids. Although these positions were hellish nightmares of inadequate pay, overwork, and frequent rape by the employer, they were the only jobs which black women could obtain. Again, racism and economics saw to it that through the unemployment of the male and the dehumanizing employment offered females, the black family suffered. During this period, the desertion rate for black males escalated. Much of what is said about the matriarchal structure of the black family began with observations that were made during this time.

When the Western African concept of respect for women is coupled with the way women were forced into positions of equal suffering during slavery, the matriarchal argument takes on a new light. The severe economic pressures of post-Reconstruction America forced blacks to adopt whatever ways were necessary to survive. "Adapt" was what blacks did to survive slavery and it was also the way after emancipation that blacks handled their plight. As demeaning as it was, if the only work available was for women to clean the master's home, it was better to do this and survive than to allow racism to destroy the family totally.

As discussed by white sociologists, matriarchy is a myth. The myth is not that female-centered homes exist. The myth is that these female-centered homes point to the male weakness. Weakness is not a word that can be used to describe either black males or females when one considers the awesome burdens that have been overcome by blacks since slavery. The only thing that the female-centered home indicates is that in the face of extraordinary pressure, the black family has somehow found the strength to survive. Jean Noble, writing in the *World Encyclopedia of Black People*, sees in all this what she calls the "myth of matriarchy."

Societal oppression, based on institutionalized efforts to keep black men subservient and dependent, deprived black men of the expected role of sole breadwinner in their families. Myths that their mothers, sisters, and wives were castrating black matriarchs simply because they were allowed to work aggravated black men's feelings of inadequacy. The fact that black women were only allowed to work at jobs which white men did not want white women to undertake became forgotten in history as the avalanche of epithets that black women were less desirable than white women. According to spokeswomen for the women's triumph over adversity, this attention is a small comfort to black women, however, because it is the respect and love of black men, and a yearning to create a partnership with them, that is paramount in black women's lives.[1]

SOCIOLOGY AND THE BLACK FAMILY

Black Americans then must not only ask, "What am I about?" but they must also ask, "What ought the family be about?" if the question of survival is to be answered. In an essay, Susanne Keller analyzes a debate on the family that took place between

---

[1]Rose Laub Coser, *The Family: Its Structure & Function*, New York. St. Martin Press, 1978), p. 579-580.

Malinowski and Briffault. She saw the difference in their opinions as resting on different definitions of the phenomenon of family."

> Malinowski defined the family as a legal union of one man and one woman with their offspring, bound by reciprocal rights and duties, cooperating for the sake of economic and moral survival. Briffault defined the family more and more broadly, as any association involving economic production and sexual procreation.[1]

Keller quotes two opinions on the formula of family. When one deals with the question of the black family, these formulas ultimately lead to the question of matriarchy. The Moynihan report of 1965 helped to fuel that fire:

> In effect, the Moynihan Report contended that low-income, urban Negro families were so unstable that equal opportunity legislation could do little to free them from "the cycle of poverty and disadvantaged" . . . In support of this position, Moynihan cited statistics from the early 1960's to the effect that, compared with white families, Negro families were more likely to be dependent on welfare assistance, to have women

---

[1]Jean Noble, "Status of the Black American Woman" in *World Encyclopedia of Black People* (St. Clair Shores, MI: Scholarly Press, 1975), p. 144.

with absentee husbands, daughters who bear illegitimate children, and high rates of crime.[1]

Charles V. Willie in his article, "Intergenerational Poverty," answers the assertions made by Patrick Moynihan in his report on the Negro family. Willie states that Moynihan's contention (that a national effort to solve the problems of Negro Americans and their family life is necessary) is based on inadequate assumptions.[2] Moynihan viewed the weakness of the family structure as the principle source of most antisocial behavior in the black community. He concludes that this "tangle of pathology" is capable of perpetuating itself. The fallacy of this, says Willie, is the assumption that values of blacks differ from values of other ethnic groups. To assume that, and to assume that this particular pathology is intergenerationally transmitted, is to assume that poverty exists only because of internal factors. To understand the black plight in America is first to be aware that internal and external factors are so interrelated that where one ends and another begins is never clearly defined.

The Malinowski-Briffault debate does seem to raise a crucial question, for the family in general as well as for black families. Can one talk about the weaknesses or strengths of the family structure unless the phenomenon of family in general is basically understood and its definitions agreed upon? Contemporary black sociologists, such as Willie, are saying that because of the uniqueness of the

---

[1]Harry A. Plosk & Ernest Kaiser, *Afro USA* (New York:, Belwether Publishing, 1967), p. 375.

[2]Charles V. Willie, *The Family Life of Black People*, (Columbus, Ohio: Charles E. Merrill, 1970), p. 316.

black struggle, questions about poverty and delinquency cannot be explained simply; a family will respond to aberrant conditions to which it must relate. Talcott Parsons, in his article, "The Normal American Family," gives the following standard formula for family:

> It can then be said that, in a sense that has probably never existed before, in a society that in most respects has undergone a process of very extensive structural differentiation, there has emerged a remarkable uniform, basic type of family. It is uniform in its kinship and household composition in the sense of confinement of its composition to members of the nuclear family, which is effective at any given stage of the family circle, and in its outside activities of its members, e.g., jobs for adult men, some participation in the labor force for women, school for children, and various others types of community participation.[1]

This kind of statement from a scholar of Parsons' magnitude constitutes a part of the confusing problem that the black family faces. Conformity to an ideal defined by the middle-class majority of America is the definition of excellence or brokenness. However, in an article entitled "The Absent Father in Negro Families: Cause or Symptom," Wasserman found in a study of the school performance of children of lower-class black families living in a low-income housing development, that there is really no external criterion for evaluating the characteristics of family life and how well it fosters educational achievement. Indeed, the scores of some

---

[1]Arlen S. Skolnick & James A. Skolnick, *Family in Transition: Rethinking Marriage.* (Boston: Little, Brown & Co., 1971), p. 397.

of the children from one-parent families were higher on scholastic and behavioral achievements than the scores of children from two-parent families.

One reason given for the stress placed upon the superiority of the two-parent nuclear family structure over any extended family models is that most Western scholars build their designs on heavily conservative, conventional models. While these scholars seem radical in their attempts to explain and understand exotic cultures, there is the very conservative thrust to justify existing institutions and practices. The dominant model of the family as it emerges in the writings of social scientists is as follows:

1. The nuclear family — a man, a woman, and their children is universally found in every human society, past and present.

2. The nuclear family is the building block of society. Larger groupings — the extended family, the clan, the society — are combinations of nuclear families.

3. The nuclear family is based on a clearcut, biological structured division of labor between man and woman, with the man playing the instrumental role of breadwinner, provider, and protector, and the woman playing the expressive role of housekeeper and emotional mainstay.

4. A major function of the family is to socialize children, that is, to tame their impulses and instill values, skills, and desires necessary to run the society.

5. Unusual family structures, such as mother and children or the experimental commune, are regarded as deviant by the participants as well as the rest of society and are fundamentally unstable and unworkable.[1]

I concede that this kind of thinking is basically enunciated in the anthropological works of Westermarch, Lowie, and Malinowski. The impact of such thinkers on the overall social science concept of the family, however, is a strong one. To hold these views is to relegate anything outside this norm to the classification of deviance. Yet the pressures of these abnormal families drastically cloud the picture so that their viability is hard to ascertain. E.E. LeMasters estimates that one in ten families in America is headed by a woman; yet, these same households constitute twenty-five percent of the so-called poverty groups in America. (Of course, this figure raises the whole question of women's comparative incomes in our society.) LeMasters figures are not just for blacks, but for all families in our society, and must be stated that the pressures of poverty-level living do seriously affect such things as higher educational pursuits. When describing the black perspective of all this, Warren D. Tenhouten stated in "The Black Family: Myth and Reality" that this assumed deviance was articulated essentially by Frazier, who describes three kinds of black families: matriarchal; the family akin to the traditional white family with the father having undisputed authority; an essentially patriarchal type originating in mixed Black, White and Indian communities; and those of mixed ancestry who define themselves as a separate, isolated race, but who were also basically patriarchal. During the great migration of blacks from the rural South to the

---

[1]Ibid., p. 3.

urban North, matriarchal families were basically unable to deal with the problems of an urban environment and resorted to charity for existence. Children ran amuck, gangs were formed, and daughters were given to a high level of illegitimate pregnancies.

Tenhouten takes exception with this thesis as being normative and also takes exception with the Moynihan report, which he considers faulty in its methodology (which assumes matriarchal dominance and male subservience). Some important points which he believes Moynihan overlooks include the following:

> One reason why black women (both poor and non-poor) are more apt to head families is a differential access to adoption. These white women who have illegitimate babies are able to have them adopted. But since the demand for black babies is low, black women have comparatively limited opportunities to have their illegitimate children adopted and thus are more apt to keep them.[1]

Secondly, he says that Moynihan's thesis implies that black men are emasculated and subdominant in their homes. "There is, however, no empirical evidence showing that black men who leave their wives do so because they are unable to play a dominant role in the family."[2] In addition, Tenhouten continues to say that there are no statistics available concerning the sixty percent of black homes with a husband present, which would indicate that these

---

[1]Ibid., p.430.

[2]Ibid., p. 430.

husbands are emasculated and subdominant in comparison to their white counterparts.

IMPLICATIONS

It is clear that there are very conservative forces within the social sciences which define the family from a very narrow perspective. Working from a post-Enlightenment mindset, these scholars are developing an image of humankind which is largely rational and individualistic. Even when the term "family" is used, it is really only used as an expanded description of the individual. The problem with definitions such as these is that they are not in keeping with the way family and relationships and individuals are defined by many non-Western cultures.

The African concept of extended family is fundamentally different from the European concept. It is based on the consanguineal rather than the conjugal unit. For this reason, black churches which are doing family enrichment must begin their work with an almost total rejection of substantive amounts of available material produced by white social scientists and theologians. Family enrichment programs for blacks can be successful only if there is a basic appreciation for the subtle yet profound differences which go into the very process of defining family.

Given the American context, there is no question that one goal of a black family enrichment program would be to shore up the strength of the nuclear family. On the other hand, the nuclear family must also be seen as fully in community with and linked to others. The results of this linkage with others can be defined as extended family if those others in the relationship share blood, or metaphorically, are linked through their shared pain, shared history, and shared hope of liberation. The black extended family is not just a gathering of nuclear families. It is a system which functions as more than the sum of its parts.

At this level, the black church has always served as an extended family. It has been to varying degrees a contemporary expression of the African consanguineal model. Within the church structure there are found both stable nuclear families and a variety of differing family models. The variances may range from one-parent families in nuclear arrangement to grandparents, uncles, aunts, or godparents serving as the primary parents for youngsters born outside the nuclear grouping.

What must be remembered is that a black family enrichment program in black churches will certainly want to work toward stable nuclear arrangements as a goal for black people. This is because the culture in which we find ourselves does not have the support systems for anything much beyond a conjugal model, and with the givens of our Western capitalist structure, young blacks will be better able to advance economically and socially if the two-parent approach is adopted. Single parents in our culture have a difficult time making it economically. Beyond that fact, however, both biblically and theologically, the two-parent model also lies at the heart of our Judeo-Christian faith. From a faith standpoint, this one fact alone means that strengthening two-parent families must be the church's goal.

On the heels of the previous statement, it must also be added that for black people a family enrichment program must not stop with the nuclear family. The nuclear family must always be seen as only a part (although an important part) of the extended family structure. All programs of family enrichment for the black church must be two-pronged. They must deal with helping to stabilize

31

two-parent families, and they must also deal with helping to enhance the extended family support network and firming up the church's ability to develop personhood and positive self-image for those trapped outside the Western accepted model of family. Women and men in one-parent relationships must be loved and nurtured. Persons living together outside of marriage must be counseled lovingly. Young people experimenting with premarital sex must be helped to respect and love themselves and their church so that they feel a kinship and affinity which will allow them the strength to avoid detrimental relationships. The elderly must be viewed as integral and functional church family members — not useless appendages. In the best concept of Paul's thoughts in Ephesians 5, mutual submissions must be the guideline for effective black family enrichment programs.

CHAPTER II

MARRIAGE — SHARING

IN THE IMAGE OF GOD

The relationships of maleness and femaleness have been a theme throughout the discussion of God's image. When one comes to the task of relating, however, other questions must be raised. Maleness and femaleness are equal portions of the original image of God shared by humanity, but interrelatedness implies a sense of covenant. It moves us from discussions of personhood to discussions of partnering, from maleness and femaleness in the abstract to male and female as individual entities.

To understand the uniqueness of partnering from a black perspective, we must examine the history and traditions of the American family. As has been mentioned, African family structure is often much more consanguineal than conjugal. For that reason, partnering in the black context must be understood much more broadly than in a purely nuclear arrangement. An African family member historically was partner in a number of arenas. There was the partnership between husband and wife, between the grandparents and children, and between the living and the dead. In fact, humankind was seen as being fully in partnership with the entirety of the created order. The African family system was marked by a general sharing within the family and between partners that was much different from the European paradigm.

The question must be raised, however, of the relationship of revelation (i.e., Scripture) to the African family system. Again, my contention is that any attempt to strengthen the black family system must take its sources from the universality of biblical truth, not from any system of philosophy or science.

34

The question, then, is what in the revelation points us toward the extended family as a model of God's interrelationship with humankind?

First, in the reality of the Trinity, we encounter a God who is in relationship with self. A basic understanding of our relationship takes on profound theological significance when God is seen as a God both of and in relationship with God's self and with the creation.

Second, the extended family concept seems to be supported by the biblical understanding of covenant. Abraham is the faithful covenant partner. It is his faithfulness which enables him to go in search of a city and have the assurance that the gods of other areas and cities had no control over him as long as his oracles were from the God who is not bound by space or of Abraham; it was also a covenant with Abraham's offspring. All his descendants who simply remained faithful to the original covenant had the profound assurance that their father's God would in turn be faithful to them.

With the coming of Christ, the concept of the extended family became even more firmly rooted in the church doctrine. Equal access to the Lord's Supper provided a way of being adopted into the family of God. Now, the membership into the family was not through blood ties but through affinity of spirit. Baptism becomes the new birth, and all who took Jesus' lordship as their point of orientation were assured that same promise of God's steadfast love as those faithful blood descendants of Abraham.

There is the biblical revelation, then, a very strong sense of extended family. This is important for the unraveling of negative stereotypes and also for the shoring up of black self-image. Female-centered families must not be automatically viewed as sick, especially when the basis of that assessment is a European nuclear family ideal. An extended family system where older brothers, uncles, or grandparents are present may provide the male role models needed to afford male and female children the nurturing necessary for proper emotional health.

Attitudes are critical in the successful implementation of any activity. This is why so much time must be spent in reestablishing the image of God in the hearts and minds of blacks throughout society.

Blacks in the Bedford Central community live consistently below the economic level of whites. The economic realities tend to exacerbate all other problems. To cope, blacks have often turned to the extended family for help. The following statement establishes a chilling reality:

> In a study, Dubey (1971) examined the relationship between self-alienation and extended family using Black, White and Puerto Rican subjects. The data supported the hypothesis that subjects with a high degree of powerlessness were significantly more oriented toward the extended family. Dubey's study raises the question of whether the extended family is used as a buffer between oppression of the dominant society and the unmet needs of the family.[1]

---

[1] Jualynne Dodson, "Conceptualizations of Black Families," p. 29 in *Black Families*, edited by Harriet McAdoo 1981, Sage Publications Inc.

Elmer P. Martin and Joanne Mitchell Martin have written a very insightful book entitled *The Black Extended Family*. The contention is ultimately that the black extended family is neither an expression of "strength resilience or of pathology disorganization"[1] but expresses both concepts. Their feeling is that the extended family model did not survive simply because the family was so broken by slavery. Nor does the extended family exist merely as a noble expression of African retention and strength resiliency. It exists as a combination of these factors, but the essential reality is that the extended family for Afro-Americans, for whatever reason, is ascendant to the nuclear arrangement.

Martin and Martin define an extended family as possessing the following characteristics:

> First, it is interdependent. Relatives depend on one another for emotional, social, and most importantly material support. Second, it is multigenerational, consisting of four generations of relatives. Third, it is headed by a dominant family figure. Fourth, it has an extended family base household, which is always the residence of the dominant family figure. Fifth, it reaches across geographical boundaries. Sixth, it has a built-in mutual aid system for providing material and moral support for family members.[2]

---

[1]Elmer P. Martin and Joanne M. Martin, *The Black Extended Family*,(Chicago: University of Chicago Press, 1978) p. 114.

[2]Ibid., p. 6

Let us examine two critical issues raised out of these definitions. First, the dominant family member is quite often a woman. This must not be used, however, as a way to denigrate the image of the black family as a matriarchy.

> A family with a female as the head appears to be a female-dominated or matriarchal household, when in fact, several male relatives may be influential in such a household setting. An uncle, a male cousin, an older brother, a boyfriend, or even a grandmother or aunt could be a father-figure to the children.[1]

Second, for Afro-American people, the extended family also acted as a mutual aid system. Economic pressures again must be weighted in every discussion of the black family. Black people from the time of slavery had first and foremost to deal with finding the resources simply to stay alive. The Kinship Network provided a way for resources to be shared. Within the family, matters of education, weddings, and health care were dealt with through the mutual sharing of a family's goods and resources.

The dominant culture's denigration of the black family system comes out of white America's romance with rugged individualism. To the conqueror of the plains and the subjugator of the Native American, a man's man was someone who took care of his family first, asked for no help and was up to whatever violence was necessary to insure that self and family dignity were not violated. The folly of that cowboy mentality is that the dominant culture

---

[2] Ibid., p. 9

was, of course, the recipient of a number of welfare programs. Slave labor certainly fits that bill. The capital generated throughout this nation through access to millions of free laborers is staggering. The thinly disguised slavery of the coolie wages paid to Orientals in the late nineteenth century was another welfare giveaway. So, too, was the original homesteading act which allowed persons to advance into entrepreneurship through the simple act of staking claim to land that was free, if you were white. It must never be forgotten that it was not rugged individualism, but theft of the land from the indigenous people through colonialism which is foundational to the power and influence of American capitalism.

The black family's mutual aid networking is not unique in this society. It was simply a carryover from Africa of a tribal structure that blacks felt comfortable with which allowed them a mutual support system. This mutual support network is of the utmost importance when it is realized that in the face of the genocide and unspeakable holocaust perpetrated against people of color, the extended family was the place blacks could turn to for support.

THE IMAGE OF GOD AND MARRIAGE

If the African extended family is to be strengthened, the sexual unions formed within the family must have some guidelines upon which to draw. Questions of matriarchy versus patriarchy must be dealt with as well as headship versus mutuality and monogamy versus polygamy. To answer these questions, let us look at some of the biblical images of marriage.

A Pharisee came up in order to test Him asked, "Is it lawful for a man to divorce his wife?" He answered them, "What did Moses command you?" They said, "Moses allowed a man to write a certificate of divorce, and to put her away." But Jesus said to them, "For your hardness of heart he wrote you this commandment. But from the beginning of creation, God made them male and female. For this reason a man shall leave his father and mother and be joined to his wife, and the two shall become one flesh." (Mark 10:2-8, RSV).

In this passage Jesus quotes the portion of the *Imago Dei* concerning maleness and femaleness. He says that from the beginning God made them His way and seems to be saying that both are co-equal aspects of the *image*. From the fact that Jesus quotes this as the goal of marriage relationships, a clear understanding of what is implied is of utmost importance. It may be recalled that the original statement of Genesis 1:26-27 (RSV) is "God said, let Us make man (adham) . . . them."

The *image* in its original conception is one of *adham*, humankind being created in the image of God. Jesus' refutation of wanton divorce laws serves as a reminder to the Pharisees that the *image* is "from the beginning." It is not something tacked on at some later date with lesser significance. It also cannot be said that the body, i.e., human sexuality, was not part of the *image* because Jesus quotes that very portion from Genesis 1:27, which asserts that maleness and femaleness are from the beginning how God made them. He then seems to say what was a radical statement: maleness and femaleness are oneness. "For this reason a man shall leave his father and mother and be joined to his wife, and the two shall become one flesh." (Mark 10:7-8, RSV). For "one" Jesus uses the Semitic idiom *mia sarx*, "one flesh."

Even though *sarx* can mean humankind generically, its use here takes on more profundity if in using the idiom for oneness, Jesus actually did intend to suggest that "fleshiness" "corporeality," has a significant slice of the image tied to it (i.e., of maleness and femaleness). There is no hard evidence to support *mia sarx* being anything but "one" but the speculation still has merit in that maleness and femaleness in the creation accounts are related to the *Imago Dei*.

Another New Testament aspect of the Imago Dei is the way it is used by Paul, especially pertaining to the notion of "headship." For the husband is the head of the wife as Christ is the head of the church, His body, and is Himself its Savior (Ephesians 5:23, RSV). With the concept of headship, Paul really says a great deal about the *Imago Dei* as he understood it. (Some of the interpretations may be startling, and it is indeed a shame that so many have undertaken work on marriage and the family without ever trying to understand what the *Imago Dei* really means to Paul's concept of headship.) To understand Ephesians 5:23 one must also have the sense of the meaning of 5:21 and 5:22.

Marcus Barth translated Ephesians 5:21 as, "Because you fear Christ." He says that this form of referring to Christ is rare in the New Testament and because of its difficult theological implications, many have shunned "fear" for a softer interpretation.

To Barth, this fear aspect solves a very basic problem; for the bridging of the gap between the rigid subordination idea of Ephesians 5:21-23 and the more universal understanding of I Corinthians 7. He goes on to say that the "haustefel" or household duties are really keyed in the concept in verse 22 of mutual subordination (that is, for husbands and wives and children); and that the mutuality of the subordination is intricately

41

entwined with a Pauline system of eschatology which is revealed more fully in I Corinthians 7.

He makes this point because his research has unearthed the fact that some manuscripts will add the imperative "subordinate yourselves" in verse 22 or "shall be subjected" as an interpretative device that unfortunately obscures the concept of mutual subjection and therefore by inference implies a natural order to male superiority and female inferiority. From this springboard, Barth makes a point which is crucial in the understanding of the *Imago Dei* (as it applies to maleness and femaleness). The literal translation "For the husband is the head of the wife as Christ is the head of the church" reduces the Messiah to a "secondary example."[1]

> Indeed, Paul could not have been ignorant of the fact that a majority of married people of this time followed a pattern of behavior which attributed superior responsibility to the husband and an inferior position to the wife; also, he must have known that this pattern was considered by many perfectly reasonable and adequate — without being informed by Jesus Christ's love for the church.[2]

The basic question here is whether or not Paul adds the relationship of Christ to the church as a superfluous addendum to

---

[1]Marcus Barth, Ephesians: *The Anchor Bible*, (Garden City: Doubleday and Co., Inc., 1974) pp. 661-662.

[2]Ibid., p. 608.

support existing customs, or did he add it to show a uniqueness, from the headship of Christ, that ought to be applied to the headship of husband over wife? If, as the New Testament passages seem to consistently imply, Christ never was given as protector of natural customs, then perhaps there is here a startling, but perceptive new understanding of headship, i.e., that "Jesus Christ is the only cause and standard for the saints' conduct," an understanding that rests on a critical interpretation of the vocabulary in the verse.

Barth translates *hos kai ho christos* in the unusual but extremely profound way as "only in Christ," which gives the fuller interpretation in this sense.

"Because you fear Christ, subordinate yourself to one another [e.g., wives to your husbands] as to the Lord. For [only] in the same way that the Messiah is the head of the church, He, the Savior of His body — is the husband, the head of his wife" (Ephesians 5:21-23).

A THEOLOGY OF MARRIAGE

At first glance, strict biblical interpretation of such passages as Ephesians 5:21-6:4 makes all but the patriarchal nuclear family (as classically defined) unacceptable. This kind of data must be understood in its broader cultural context; and just as no one of any degree of intelligence would accept the definition of the master-slave relationship in these passages as normative and desirable, the existence of present-day cultural considerations must also weigh on the strict interpretation of the husband-wife dyad as the ideal for family life, the counter notion that all other family experience is deviant and therefore unstable is an unacceptable thesis. The spirit of these passages and their intent seems to lie in the basic assumption that the quality of life is made better by a relationship with Christ that allows for total subjection to the needs of others and total respect for the uniqueness of others. God intends for Christians to live in unity, which Paul seems to be saying in Ephesians 4:1-6, and this is done by the nurturing of all the specific gifts of those who are members of the body. In Galatians 3:26-28 (RSV), we find, "For in Christ Jesus you are all sons of God, through faith. For as many of you as were baptized into Christ have put on Christ. There is neither Jew nor Greek, there is neither slave nor free, there is neither male nor female; for you are all one in Christ Jesus."

What he is stating for women is that there is to be new status found in Christ Jesus. That analogy can be carried over into the family structure. For the Christian family there is new life in Christ Jesus, new life which does not place the excellency of any given family on adherence to roles, but places its excellency on the strengthened relationships of those family members who have mutually subjected themselves to Christ, mutually pledged respect for their own specific uniqueness, and mutually worked toward the building of positive self-images.

For many, however, the passage in Ephesians is a troubling one: "For the husband is the head of the wife as Christ is the head of the church, His body, and is Himself its Savior (5:23, RSV). The passage at first reading seems uncomfortable because it seems to state so definitively Paul's concept of the husband-wife relationship. Heinrich Schlier, in the *Theological Dictionary of the New Testament*, looks at the Greek word which is translated as "head." He says that the head is not present without or apart from the body, nor the body without or apart from the head. The church is the earthly body of the heavenly head. In this unity of Christ and the church, the of Christ headship is manifested in the fact that He directs the growth of the body to Himself. This understanding makes critical the idea of growth. The head determines the being of the body and the fulfillment of its life. As the head, Christ is the concrete principle of the bodily growth of the church. Schlier's definition, when applied to the present-day family, would remove the essentiality of economic viability in a definition of the man as the head of the family. Growth of the unit and wholeness of the family unit are not contingent upon the economic leadership of the male. The translation of Marcus Barth of Ephesians 5:23 adds a great deal of insight to the question of headship. Barth's translation provides a radical break from the legalistic and pagan perspectives of headship implying patriarcate, i.e., male dominance. The husband is head "only" as Christ is head, and Christ's headship is not demonstrated by dominance but by subjection, both to others and to God.

45

This also adds a fresh perspective to the account in Mark 10:2-8. The question is not the power question of whether or not husbands have the right to put away their wives. The question is the love ethic question, resolved by maleness and femaleness being a part of the "image of God," co-equal, co-responsible, and co-dependent upon each other.

A family is not matriarchal simply because it does not meet certain standards. It is not broken simply because the male is not in the position of economic leadership. Black sociologists have repeatedly taken the position that the black male's economic frailty is not based on inherent ineptness or inaptitude; it is instead based on a rigorous racism that has permeated all levels of the American culture psyche, as is demonstrated by the monthly unemployment statistics.

The most striking feature of African family and community life was the strong and dominant place in family and society assigned to and assumed by the men. This strong, masculine dominance, however, far from being capricious authoritarianism, was supported, guided, and limited by custom and tradition which also provided a substantial role for the women. The children were provided a quality of care and protection not common in modern society, for they belonged not alone to their father and mother, but also and principally, to the wider kinship group.[1]

In *Man as Male and Female*, Paul K. Jewett explored an idea that helps to focus the whole question (theologically) of male-female interdependence.

---

[1]Andrew Billingsley, *Black Families in White America* (Englewood Cliffs, New Jersey: Prentice Hall, 1968) p. 40.

There are, broadly speaking, three schools of thought about the sexual polarity of man's existence, which are neglected at least to some degree, in representative Christian writers. First of all, there is the position that the male-female distinction has nothing to contribute to our understanding of man as created in the divine image. A second view affirms that while the male-female distinction is not an essential part of the doctrine of man, it is evident from Scripture that both male and female share the distinct endowments whereby man differs from animals; that is to say that men and women both participate in the divine image. According to a third view, to be in the image of God is to be male and female.[1]

Nicholai Berdyaev, a writer holding to the first view, feels that the polar nature of maleness and femaleness is due to humanity's fallen nature. He sees human fulfillment only in the union of the personal anthropological principles which are masculine with the communal and cosmic principles which are feminine. A theologian of the more traditional second view is Emil Brunner, who treats the question of man as male and female. "Brunner does not have a theology of sexuality which would make the man/woman distinction essential to humanity."

Brunner's anthropology really sees sexuality, and not marriage, as the touchstone of the male-female question. His theology merges the question of what the Christian understanding is of man as male and female with the question of what the Christian understanding is of the roles which the male and female have to fill respectively in the ordinance of marriage. His answer

---

[1]Paul K. Jewett, *Man as Male and Female* (Grand Rapids: Erdman, 1975) p. 24.

is that sexual dualism is neither to be played down nor glorified. The ultimate fulfillment is the life to come when we shall forever be like God, with emphasis being placed on Mark 12:25. "At the resurrection of the dead they neither marry nor are given in marriage, but are like the angels in heaven" (paraphrased).

The third view, as articulated by Marcus Barth, assumes that the concept of man and woman is tied to the concept of the *Imago Dei*. Genesis 1:27 (RSV) says, "So God created man in his own image, in the image of God created he him, male and female created he them." Barth's position is that we never say "mankind" without having to say either "man" or "woman." Man has his existence based precisely on this distinction. In all human uniqueness, persons are still either male or female.

Man is male and female, and the concept of man in the image of God lies in that unity. Sexuality is not some incidental footnote to life; it is the core existence in marriage one side of this duality has no meaning without the concurrent other side. Marcus Barth, much more than some other theologians, has developed a doctrine which forces one to develop a theology of man which is also a theology of woman.

While in a Nazi prison camp, Dietrich Bonhoeffer wrote a wedding sermon which captures the richness of the concept of responsibility in marriage to each other but also of responsibility to humankind:

> "Marriage is more than your love for each other.
> It has a higher dignity and power, for it is God's
> holy ordinance through which He wills to
> perpetuate the human race until the end of time.
> In your love, you see only your two selves in the

world, but in marriage you are a link in the chain of generations, which God causes to come and to pass away to His glory, and calls into His kingdom. In your love you see only the heaven of your happiness, but in marriage you are placed at the post of responsibility towards the world and its making. Your love is your own private possession, but marriage is more than something personal — it is a status, an office.[1]

The points that Bonhoeffer raises are important. Christian marriage does have a profound significance and sanctity. The New Testament is moving us to see how the progressive nature of God's revelation has reached a zenith for interpersonal communication in the office of marriage. Unlike the ancient customs, Christian marriage forces persons to see women not as chattel but as full participators in the original image of God. Therefore, women are not to be treated as objects or believed to exist simply to satisfy men. Christian marriages raised women to a level of dignity which was unheard of in antiquity.

Christian marriage lifts up mutual sacrifice as the *sine quo non* of human relations. Marriage is to reflect the mutual subjection that demands of each partner full loving sacrifice to the other. This does not mean that individuality is lost. It means that a new sense of identity is found when one is willing to give totally. Much as the carpenter from Nazareth became Jesus the Christ through His obedience unto the cross, in mutual sacrifice persons are transformed into a unique oneness of body and mind.

---

[1]Quoted in L. Christenson, *The Christian Family* (Minneapolis: Bethany Fellowship, 1970) p. 9.

Marriage requires that persons pledge themselves in full trust to the other. This cannot be done as an ideal notion. It must be done with full understanding that by pledging one's self, one is also pledging one's life.

As Bonhoeffer points out, this new shared sense of responsibility is an office. By accepting the responsibility of marriage one is showing that he or she is accepting a unique but vital responsibility. By the same token, a single lifestyle is not second-class citizenship. There is a nobility which also can be a part of a single life if other aspects of mutual responsibility are accepted. The genius of the extended family permits that possibility.

The office of marriage, however, is an office in which two persons accept the church's sanction to bring new life into the world. At this point the marital office is indeed unique and its responsibilities of a different order than that of the single person.

This Christian marriage is marked biblically by pure mutuality, sacrifice, love (in its highest form) and exclusivity. These concepts all culminate in the doctrine of one flesh.

GOD AND FEMALE/MALE RELATIONSHIPS

In attempting to establish revelation as the basis of a theology of the black family, the question of female/male interrelatedness must be raised. The extended family concept not withstanding, one must come to grips with the image of God as it relates to males and females and the nature of the marital covenant. A knowledge and appreciation of the consanguineal family structure of western Africa has tremendous potential to help and to heal black families. A knowledge of one's roots, as Alex Haley brilliantly displayed, is a very liberating phenomenon. On the heels of that knowledge of history, however, blacks must also have a deep appreciation for the directions in which God's revelation is pointing. Ultimately and finally there is no authentic liberation outside of God's revelation.

The image of God is rounded out as an image of male-female interrelatedness. Individually we are both male and female, but each of us also specifically male or female. God's revelation clearly points to male-female monogamous relationships as the gift given by God to humankind for the purposes of procreation and nurturing. Even for people of African descent, this concept of monogamy must be at the heart of even the extended family structure.

For African peoples, the polygamous system grew up out of the frequent wars that insured that female survival rates were higher than male. Polygamy was a way of insuring that women would not become spinsters and therefore lose the potential for child hearing. Polygamy was also a way of preventing a proliferation of prostitution.

The rather high rate of common-law marriage among blacks in this country is a vestige of the African polygamous system. Some in the country today still argue for polygamy as an alternative to the deliberate murder practice upon black people and to the still much higher rates of eligible females to males because of the disproportionately high percentages of black males who are imprisoned, compared to their ethnic composition in American society. Such practices are seen as necessary for the survival of a people.

These problems are problems which certainly must be dealt with, but an understanding of the revelation of God certainly indicates that polygamous marriages are not a part of the created image of God. Male and female in a deep and abiding partnership is the only authentic way that one can read Genesis 1:26-27. When other lifestyles are adopted outside of the male/female, it must be understood that those lifestyles do not reflect the clearest response that can be given. Black leaders, teachers, and preachers must be about the task of developing national strategies that deal with the need for drastic prison reforms as well as better nutrition, better prenatal care, and effective job training for the developing job markets as ways of improving the black birth rate and insuring that blacks have equal access to a fair share of the American dream. That kind of leadership must be performed at the same time that monogamous, committed marriage is being taught. Only when blacks have the opportunity to align themselves totally with God's intentions will liberation develop into an actual possibility.

CHAPTER III

BIBLICAL UNDERSTANDING

OF MARRIAGE

INTRODUCTION

A significant part of the conceptual basis for this thesis-project is found in the Old and New Testaments. As a cursory reading of the Bible will indicate, there are no specific passages or models that deal with conflict management for married couples per se. Nevertheless, there are general references throughout the Bible to such related areas as the marriage relationship, interpersonal conflict, human anger, verbal communication, etc. By examining passages such as these, it is expected that certain basic principles can be abstracted and applied to the present thesis-project.

Topics to be covered are: (1) Marriage in the Bible, (2) A Theology of Conflict, (3) The Matter of Anger, (4) Methods of Handling Conflict, (5) A Formula for Growth in Conflict and (6) Summary. All biblical quotations are from the Revised Standard Version unless otherwise noted. The Masoretic Text of the Old Testament edited by Kittel[1] and the Greek New Testament edited by Aland, et al,[2] are used for the purpose of exegeses.

---

[1]Rud, Kittel, ed., *Biblia Heraica*, 3rd ed. (Stuttgart, West Germany: Privileg. Wurt, Bibelanstalt, 1954).

[2]Kurt Aland et al, eds. *The Greek New Testament*, 2nd ed. (Stuttgart, West Germany: Wurttemberg Bible Society, 1968).

MARRIAGE IN THE BIBLE

In the Old Testament, the form of marriage shows a cultural progression from polygamy to monogamy. The actual practice of polygamy is most evident from the patriarchal period to the United Kingdom. The law in Deuteronomy, however, demands of the king that "he shall not multiply wives for himself, lest his heart turn away" (Deuteronomy 17:17). Monogamous fidelity is further stressed by the prophets and is used symbolically of the marital-like union between God and Israel, which was broken by the harlotry of Israel's apostasy. It is this view that in the New Testament, that monogamy is assumed to be the general rule.[1] Jesus affirms the "one-flesh" idea of creation as ordained of God and to be respected. Paul likewise supports the same concept in his reference to marriage and the record of creation. Thus in the Bible, monogamy occupies a prominent position, especially in those passages that are important to the understanding of marriage.[2]

The nature of the marital relationship in Scripture is strongly masculine or patriarchal. In the account of the fall, Adam is to rule over his wife Eve (Genenis 3:16). The Decalogue lists a wife among a man's possessions along with his servants and animals. A woman passes from the dominion of her father to that of her husband whom he gives in marriage. The husband is called "master" (ba al) by his wife in the Hebrew text (Genesis 20:3). A husband could even nullify a wife's vows if he felt so inclined. In

---

[1] *Dict Theological ionary of the New Testament*, 1964 ed., s.v. "yuvn," by Albrecht Oepke, p. 305.

[2] *The New International Dictionary of New Testament Theology*, 1976 ed., s.v. Marriage," by W. Gunther, p. 49.

I Corinthians 11:3, Paul states, "The head of a woman is her husband," and a similar viewpoint is repeated in several other epistles as well. Subordination thus appears to be the traditional position of a wife in the Bible.

There are several biblical references that support a mutual and equal relationship between men and women. In the Genesis account of creation, for example, it is stated that both male and female are created equally in the image of God. Both man and woman are also to exercise equal lordship over the natural world (Genesis 1:27). Marriage is described as a covenant relationship between the two partners. In Mark 10:11, Jesus recognized that a wife as well as a husband can dissolve a marriage. While in I Corinthians 7:4 Paul teaches that a wife has rule over her husband's body and vice versa, both spouses are to submit themselves to one another in fear of God. But undoubtedly, the strongest statement on equality is that "there is neither male nor female; for you are all one in Christ" (Galatians 3:18).

The aforementioned Scriptures give two explanations for the purpose of marriage: procreative and unitive. In the (Genesis 1:27) creation narrative, the specific reason for marriage is procreativity, e.g. "be fruitful and multiply." The admonition of procreation is repeated three more times to Noah's family and to Jacob. According to the other creation narrative, (Genesis 2:21-23) the stated purpose is unitive, e.g., "one flesh." The New Testament emphasizes the unitive, but not the procreative purpose of marriage. The emphasis on unity in marriage is due to the precedence that both Jesus and Paul give to the "one flesh" concept. Paul further employs the unitive conception of marriage as an analogy of Christ's union with the church (II Corinthians 11:2). Consequently, the unitive purpose of marriage is the dominant in the Bible, having figurative and theological usage as well.

The opposite to this unitive purpose of marriage is the painful reality of divorce. Divorce is not the optimal solution to marital conflict; rather, God desires that marriage partners remain together (Mark 10:9). Implied by various passages is the development of a mutual relationship on the part of a couple to cope with marital issues. The Mosaic code did not permit divorce and remarriage when a man found "some indecency" in his wife (Deuteronomy 24:1). By contrast, Jesus advocated an indissoluble union, conceding divorce only on account of adultery, but not commending remarriage even in that case. As Achtemeier says, "Jesus tells us that divorce and infidelity are wrong, that God wants our marriages to last a lifetime."[1] It would be my understanding that were Jesus present today domestic violence would be at the top of His list for dissolving a marriage relationship. Jesus' actions and words were explicit concerning how people should be treated and His emphasis was on the equality of male and female relationships. There is no doubt in my mind that Jesus' behavior and words superseded a cultural norm of the time and should be the practice of Christians today. From a biblical perspective then, marriage is to be monogamous in form and mutual in nature.

---

[1]Elizabeth Achtemeier, *The Committed Marriage* (Philadelphia: Westminster Press, 1976), p. 120.

A THEOLOGY OF CONFLICT

John J. Lally and Robert B. Lauric are two authors who present a theology of conflict that bears attention in this book. Lally's perspective is primarily from the New Testament, while Lauric's is basically from the Old Testament. Lally begins his presentation by questioning the false assumption that conflict is always the work of the devil, whereas peace is the sole ministry of Christ.[1] By contrast, his basic thesis is that interpersonal conflict is integral to the Christian mission, message, and life, and that the avoidance or stifling of such conflict is often a sign of immaturity and a block to the work of the Holy Spirit. This position he believes is supported by the life of Christ, the teaching of Christ, and the witness of the rest of the New Testament.

Christ is the central figure in the realm of Christian conflict. His life is marked by conflict from birth to death. There is evident tension between Him and His family, His followers, and His religious opponents. The large majority of the parables focus on conflict in content and context. Christ's teaching is a paradox between peace and conflict and offers an inner peace on one hand and interpersonal conflict on the other. Eschatologically, there is conflict not peace, e.g., "Do not think that I have come to bring peace on earth; I have not come to bring peace, but a sword" (Mark 10:34). Those disciples who bear witness to Christ are warned to expect antagonism and even persecution, but they are still to persist in the struggle for truth by the aid of the Spirit. Excellent illustrations of the understanding of this in the early

---

[1]John J. Lally, "A Theology of Conflict," in *New Testament Themes for Contemporary Man*, ed. Rosalie M. Ryan (Englewood Cliffs, New Jersey: Prentice Hall, Inc., 1969), p. 161.

church are found in the post-Pentecostal activities of the apostles as recorded in Acts, and in the mission of Paul to the Gentiles.

Christian conflict is not limited just to those outside the people of God. There are also struggles within the church and among individual believers. The theological issues discussed at the Jerusalem Council, as well as Paul's confrontation with Peter over Jewish observances are good examples. Even family tensions, where one's foes are of his own household are suggested by Jesus from an eschatological perspective. Yet the presence of conflict does not signify the lack of love. "Indeed, love of neighbor often requires the Christian to enter into conflict with others in the church."[1] Certainly, Christ was not uncharitable in confronting others; He acted out of an imperative of love to challenge them to respond appropriately in faith. Love does not always require harmony, and unity is not always achieved by conformity. In fact, "it requires more effort to approach conflict in a spirit of love than it does to establish or preserve peaceful relations."[2]

Lally considers nonviolence as the Christian way, but is not convinced that violence by the Christian is never called for, at least as the lesser of two evils. Interpersonal conflict is valid whenever it is necessary or expedient, and is compatible with the spirit of Christ; but not when it is for its own sake, the product of willed hatred, without love for the other, or just offensively personal. He further suggests that the perfect peace of Christ is eschatological, that is, in a continuing process toward realization. "Harmony in human relations inevitably alternates with conflict in a kind of

---

[1]Ibid., p. 165

[2]Ibid., p. 167

dialectic-conflict always involving striving toward a new harmony, which itself is subject to change through further striving and conflicts — but that a certain abiding interior peace, even in the midst of conflict, is possible."[1] One cannot escape the fact that, as a Christian, a person must have the courage to face life and act, whether the action requires a conflicting or peaceful encounter with others.

Lauric defines conflict from a theological perspective as "the struggle against all the diminishing forces of life, in order to bring about the achievement of God's purposes for the world."[2] This achievement of God's purpose most simply means a better life in a better world. The whole idea is to bring about a new life for one's self and others. With that kind of goal in mind, Christian conflict must therefore be categorized as constructive or creative conflict. "Conflict is not good in itself, but always to be creative of something else — a more ordered, interdependent, fulfilled self.[3] That is why the various characters of the Bible were willing to accept pain and conflict in order to obtain such higher objectives. It also accounts for the fact that throughout Scripture there is the promise of peace over and against the reality of conflict to reach that state.

Concerning the first part of the definition, Lauric states that "a diminishing force is anything — whether it's mental or spiritual or

---

[1]Ibid., p. 168

[2]Robert B. Lauric, *Conflict: A Biblical Perspective* (Pasadena, Calif.: Associates in Human Communication, 1974), p. 3.

[3]Ibid., p. 6

psychological or physical — anything that destroys or detracts from a person's interdependence with God, with the natural world, and with others."[1] A diminishing force is appropriately classified as sin, and sin is any destructive act or attitude that keeps a person from the relationship or interdependence which brings about the kind of life God intends. For this project, the emphasis would be on the interdependence or interpersonal relationship with a significant other, one's spouse, to achieve the kind of marriage that the marital union is supposed to be. Conflict would then result as any diminishing force to the marriage or couple is encountered.

The social message of the prophets is seen by Lauric as person-centered and their prophetic critique as directed against the person diminishing elements of society.[2] Prophets like Amos were not so much interested in developing a particular kind of society as they were in helping the individual become a whole person regardless of the social system. Three significant aspects of interpersonal concern are attributed to the prophets: (1) the individual needs recognition of his uniqueness; (2) the individual needs to be responsible for the community and (3) the individual needs freedom from the community.[3] What is applicable here to the larger unit of society may also be applied to the smaller unit of marriage. Conflict may likewise occur in the context of marriage when a spouse's uniqueness or personal identity is lost, when one partner fails to be responsible for the other, and when the freedom to be destroyed by the bond of marital union.

---

[1] Ibid., p. 4

[2] Ibid., p. 4

[3] Ibid., p. 4-5

Biblical conflict for Lauric is to be undertaken voluntarily in face of the full range of pain it entails in order to overcome the disorders of life.[1] He distinguishes this voluntary nature of conflict from mere accident or misfortune where similar pain is really beyond one's control, and from punishment where such suffering is actually a penal consequence. The personal attainment of peace requires this kind of voluntary struggle. Peace is something one struggles to achieve; it is not something that is just there. The Hebrew word "peace" (shalom) comes from a root meaning to finish or to complete. Appropriately, Lauric defines peace as "accomplished well-being."[2] For him, shalom or peace is accomplished well-being through struggle, not apart from it. Such peace is not the absence of conflict but the absence of fear in conflict; it is a sense of being able to overcome and change for the better.

The reason for conflict in the opinion of Lauric is twofold: the nature of the world; and the purpose of persons.[3] The nature of the world is such that it is unfinished, incomplete, and still in process. He notes that Genesis 2:3 leaves the seventh day incomplete in that there is no terminal formula as in the other six days, e.g., "and there was evening and there was morning. . ." (Genesis 1:5,8,13,19,23,31). This depicts the incompleteness of the world which is seen as one reason for conflict. Conflict is thus inevitable because the world is in a struggle for completion and change is imperative in the process of growth. The purpose of

---

[1]Ibid., p. 6

[2]Ibid., p. 7

[3]Ibid., p. 8-9

persons described in Genesis 1:28 is to fill the earth and to subdue it. Here to subdue the earth is taken to mean to bring it into order, confront it, enter in conflict with it. Humankind is to work creatively with God to subdue and to complete the world. Conflict is therefore integral to life and an order of creation. To withdraw from conflict then is to risk sinning against this order of creation.[1] Again, I believe there are some limits to conflict and this writer clearly believes that one does not have a responsibility to remain in a conflict situation such as domestic violence.

According to a theological perspective, conflict is thus viewed as both an integral and an inevitable part of life. It is not to be destructive, but constructive in scope and outcome. Such conflict is to be undertaken voluntarily in full view of the consequences and out of a sense of love for others. To withdraw from conflict that is expedient or necessary, may block the work of the Holy Spirit and be an occasion of sin. Conflict and peace are dialectic and stand in paradox, for real peace is accomplished well-being through conflict. These same principles are also equally applicable to marital conflict.

THE MATTER OF ANGER

One of the important factors in the course of conflict is anger. Anger is the result of those feelings and expressions of antipathy toward an object, which are aroused by a sense of injury or wrong, inducing a reaction from mild resentment to destructive violence.[2]

---

[1] Ibid., p. 9

[2] Ibid., p. 2

In Scripture, anger is ascribed to both humankind and God, but there is a definite distinction between human and divine anger. The difference is that anger per se is not considered a specific characteristic of God, but rather a matter of retributive justice.[1] God's anger is a holy wrath directed against sin. It stems essentially from God's attribution of righteousness which demands justice and judgment, in face of injustice and unrighteousness. Thus God's wrath also justifies a limited or appropriate anger in the human sphere; otherwise, all anger has to be condemned without exception.[2] The biblical assessment of human anger is not uniform. For example, some of the earlier parts of the Old Testament describe anger in a neutral or even positive sense. It is seen as one of the characteristic elements of human behavior that has to be taken seriously when encountered and has to be coped with prudently. There is actually a certain dignification of the human capacity for and exercise of anger. But in many of the later sections of the Old Testament, outbursts of anger are considered as a vice and unwise. It is the wisdom literature, especially the book of Proverbs, that gives the strongest negative evaluation (Proverb 14:29). Destructive not constructive anger is the main concern, and thus it is to be avoided. The antithesis is between the angry person and the wise person, it is between being short tempered and long suffering.

Most references in the New Testament to human anger are negative due to a destructive connotation. In the case of Jesus,

---

[1]Ibid., p. 9

[2]*Theological Dictionary of the New Testament*, 1964 ed., s.v. "opyn," by Johannes Fichtner.

however, His anger is viewed more as a manifestation of divine wrath than human emotion. Two very positive references to human anger are found in Romans 10:19 and II Corinthians 7:11. The former relates to anger induced of God and the latter to well-founded anger at wrong doing.[1] Two verses also concede to the possibility of appropriate anger: James 1:19, where one is to be slow to anger, and Ephesians 4:26-27, where one is to be quick to overcome it. Essentially then in the New Testament, destructive anger is condemned, while appropriate anger may be conceded as a possibility. "Anger, while very likely to become sinful, is not really sinful in itself."

Ephesians 4:26-27 is probably the most significant passage towards a psychology for dealing constructively with anger, and the one reference on anger that needs to be considered exegetically for purposes of this book. The verses read: "Be angry but not sin; do not let the sun go down on your anger, and give no opportunity to the devil." (Ephesians 4:26-27).

The main theological concept of Ephesians is unity in Christ through the church, while the purpose of the practical section is instruction for living in Christ. The verses under consideration are part of the practical section and specifically the exhortation to be done with pagan ways (Ephesians 4:17-5:20). It is one of the special injunctions of Ephesians 4:25-5:2, where previous attitudes and actions are contrasted to life and Christ.

Therefore, the biblical record does teach that a limited or appropriate anger is justified in both the divine and human realm.

---

[1]Theological Dictionary of the New Testament, "opyn."

Human anger is regarded as a passionate emotion which is to be taken seriously and coped with prudently. Anger in itself is not sinful, but quite often becomes so. It is this kind of destructive anger that is to be avoided and that is classified as a vice. In Ephesians 4:26-27, the principle is that anger can be aroused justly but must be resolved before the day is over lest it becomes sinful anger. The application to marital conflict would be that appropriate anger is justifiable but must be dealt with constructively on a day-to-day basis lest it becomes destructive and ends in hurtful hostility.

CHAPTER IV

METHODS OF

HANDLING CONFLICT

Before I can define conflict resolution, I must first define the word conflict. According to Boardman and Horowitz (1994, p. 3) conflict is an incompatibility of behaviors, cognition (including goals), and/or affect among individuals or groups that may or may not lead to an aggressive expression of this social incompatibility. Heitler (1990, p. 5) defines conflict as a situation in which seemingly incompatible elements exert force in opposing or divergent directions. The World Book Encyclopedia Dictionary (1983) defined conflict as a fight or struggle, especially a long one; a battle.

Conflict has existed since humans were first on the earth. According to one's belief about the creation of the world, conflict can be found from the beginning. I will discuss conflict in terms of the scientific view of evolution, and the Bible, popular literature studied in this institution and other academic institutions. Conflict can occur internally in an individual, or externally amongst two people, groups, or countries on the largest scale. I will begin to look at the history and the origins of conflict according to the three sources as I have mentioned above.

The history of conflict according to the scientific explanation of evolution began in the very beginning. Since the dawn of history, people have fought against people (The World Book Encyclopedia, 1982, volume 21, p. 21). The first tool or weapon that ancient man discovered was fire, around the year 500,000 B.C. Fire was used to provide warmth and also as a way to keep the animals away. Obviously, conflict is not limited to human against human only, for it can include human versus animal.

68

The club was probably the first tool which prehistoric man used besides fire. Other weapons which he used to settle conflicts included the bow and arrow, and the spear thrower. The first history of conflict in war is said to have occurred when King Menes of Upper Egypt conquered Lower Egypt in 3100 B.C. The history of conflict in Greece can be traced back to 1450 B.C. when Greeks from the mainland captured the island of Knossos. Throughout the history of Greece, they have conquered other lands, which is a form of conflict. In 546 B.C., Cyrus the Great conquered Asia Minor. Egypt had been invaded several times by foreigners. Sheshonk I, a Libyan, seized the Egyptian throne at about 945 B.C. (The World Book Encyclopedia, 1982, volume 6, p. 100) A Sudanese leader overthrew the Libyans after 200 years of Libyan rule, and the Sudanese were overthrown by the Assyrians after ruling for 85 years.

There is quite a history of wars which have occurred in both the countries of ancient Egypt and Ancient Greece. Between 146 and 27 B.C., the Romans completed the task of conquering Greece. Much of the history of conflict in the world has centered around religion. The three main religions that have been in constant conflict are Judaism, Islam, and Christianity. Islam and Christianity were formed from the Judaic religion. Each of these religions has attempted to spread to other regions in order to convert others. Islam was the first religion to spread across the world. Islamic civilization, in contrast, was the first that can be called universal, in the sense that it comprised people of many different races and cultures on three different continents (Lewis, p.10).

Islam existed in Spain, southern Italy, the Russian Steppes and the Balkan Peninsula. Since Muhammad started his mission in seventh century Arabia, and the expansion his followers made into the Mediterranean world, Islam became the enemy and rival of Christendom. Both religions believed in doing whatever it took to spread their messages. The Muslims have a term called a *jihad*, which is essentially a war. The Christians used the term crusades to signify the spread of their faith.

The very first Islamic expansion took place largely at Christian expense: Syria, Palestine, Egypt, and North Africa were all Christian countries or provinces of the Christian Roman Empire or subject to other Christian rulers, until they were incorporated in the realm of the caliphs (Lewis, 1995, p.11). The Muslim faith expanded into Europe three times; the first time being in the early eighth century. This expansion engulfed Spain, Portugal, southern Italy and even parts of France. This expansion ended in 1942. These lands were taken back by the Christians for the most part. On January 2, 1942, the combined armies of Ferdinand of Aragon and Isabella of Castille recaptured Grenada from the Muslims.

The history of conflict among the Jewish people, the Christian people, and the Muslim people is not confined to the 15th century, for it continues today in many regions of the world. Conflicts where religion is still the major decisive issue can be seen in Bosnia, Northern Ireland, and the Middle East. In Northern Ireland, the conflict is taking place between different factions of Christians. These conflicts have the potential of escalating to the point where they might break out to create a major international incident.

A famous conflict that took place between two men in the early part of the history of the United States occurred between Alexander Hamilton and Aaron Burr. This conflict centered around politics. It started when there was a tie in the voting for the presidency in 1800 between Thomas Jefferson and Aaron Burr.

Alexander Hamilton used his influence to convince the House of Representatives to break the tie in Jefferson's favor. When Burr ran for governor of New York in 1804, Hamilton worked to help Burr be defeated. Burr lost the election and challenged Hamilton to a duel. They fought on July 11, 1804, and Hamilton was shot and killed by Burr with one single shot.

The biggest internal conflict that the United States experienced was the Civil War. The Civil War started on April 12, 1861, and ended on April 9, 1865. There were many issues that led up to the start of the fighting between the North and the South. Many persons call this tragic conflict the War Between the States, the War of the Rebellion, the War of the Secession, or the War for Southern Independence (The World Book Encyclopedia, 1982, volume 4. p.472). The Civil War took more American lives than any other war in the history of the country.

The bloodiest, most costly and destructive international conflict in the history of modern times was World War II. World War II lasted from September 1939 to September 1945. The three main causes of World War II were: (1) the problems left unsolved by World War I; (2) the rise of dictatorships; and (3) the desire of Germany, Italy, and Japan for more territory. (The World Book Encyclopedia, 1982, volume 21, p. 381) One thing evident from World War II is that the strategy of conflict avoidance or appeasement is not always the best way to avoid conflicts.

Another decisive conflict that affected America internally was the Vietnam War. This conflict which originally started between the North and the South in Vietnam became a major struggle. In the United States, the country was divided as to whether its soldiers should be sent to take part in this disagreement. This conflict was caused to a large extent by political ideology. The division that the Vietnam War caused in the United States can still be felt today.

There have been many more international conflicts that have occurred since the Vietnam War. Some of these have been the dispute between Great Britain and Argentina over the Falkan Islands; the continuing conflict between Israel and its Arab neighbors over territory; and the Soviet Union's invasion of Afghanistan; the Iraqi invasion of Kuwait which resulted in Operation Desert Storm; the United Nations' intervening in Somalia and Haiti; the incident that took place in China at Tianamen Square involving an uprising over the resistance to Communism and an attempt to introduce some democratic reforms.

The earliest source of conflict that I have located in the Bible appears in Genesis 3. Conflict first occurred in the Bible when Eve was tempted to eat from the forbidden tree. The next example of conflict occurs when Cain slew his brother Abel because of jealousy. This is a perfect example of where conflict resolution or conflict management techniques were needed. Another example of conflict in the Bible occurred between Esau and his brother Jacob, the sons of Isaac. The conflict there was over Esau's birthright as the first son. This ended up being settled peacefully. Jacob used several techniques including offering himself as his brother's servant to settle the dispute.

One of the biggest occurrences of conflict in the Bible involved David and Goliath, in I Samuel 17. This took place during the battle between the Philistines and Israel. This is an example of conflict leading to a battle between people of different lands. David experienced further conflict after he became King of Israel, which is an example of internal conflict. Consequently,

David was led to betray his most faithful servant because he desired the servant's wife, Bathsheba.

There are also many other examples of conflict found in the Bible, and I'll mention just a few more here. In I Kings 3:17-28, the event involved the dispute of two women over a child, and this conflict was resolved by the mediation of King Solomon. Then there is evidence of conflict between Samson and Delilah. We find that the Philistines wanted to gain revenge against Samson and they used Delilah to find out his weakness. Delilah betrayed Samson, and when he was captured by the Philistines his eyes were put out. In the end, Samson — by God's aid — temporarily regained his strength and was able to pull down two pillars, killing many of the Philistines and himself.

There is also conflict evident in the Bible among the sons of Jacob. This incident centered around the jealousy which the brothers felt towards their younger brother, Joseph. The events of this conflict begin in Genesis 37:7, and this was not settled peacefully at all for a while. The brothers were jealous of Joseph because he was their father's favorite son, for he was also the father's youngest son. The brothers' jealousy festered until they first threw him in a well, leaving him to die; and then they sold him into slavery to some Egyptians.

Another example of conflict is throughout the book of Exodus. The conflict here deals with the refusal of the Pharaoh to let the people of Israel leave Egypt. The people of Israel were slaves and constantly were tormented because they out-numbered the Egyptians. Moses, the leader of the Israelites, appeared on behalf of the people and appealed to the Pharaoh to release the people so that they could go into the promised land and worship the Lord. However, Pharaoh refused this request time and time again. God brought many tragedies upon the people of Egypt before the Pharaoh finally released the people. One of the tragedies involved the killing of the firstborn of all the Egyptians. Finally, after this tragedy the Pharaoh let the Israelites leave. This conflict is recorded in Exodus 12:29.

As we turn to the New Testament Scriptures, there are also other examples of conflict, starting with the birth of Jesus Christ. When Jesus was born, Herod the King became fearful because of the prophecies which proclaimed Christ as King of the Jews. Herod sent out three wise men to find the infant Jesus so that he could have him killed. Joseph, Mary's husband, having been warned by angels of Herod's plan in a dream, departed into Egypt with Mary and the infant Jesus. This potential conflict was avoided by Joseph fleeing the country with his family. This can be found in the Scriptures in St. Matthew 2:13.

One way in which Christ encouraged the handling of conflict can be found in St. Matthew 5:38-44. The way in which Jesus commanded the conflict be handled was "Ye have heard that it hath been said, 'an eye for an eye, and a tooth for a tooth,' but I say unto you, that ye resist not evil; but whosoever shall smite thee on thy right cheek, turn to him the other also."

There is an example of internal conflict starting with Matthew 26:33. The conflict here is when Peter denied being one of the disciples of Christ because he feared reprisal. Then there is internal conflict evident with Judas Iscariot, the man who betrayed Jesus. Judas having betrayed Christ and receiving his reward from the chief priests, was condemned in his internal conflict and threw down the pieces of silver and hanged himself. As the Scripture reads, "And he cast down the pieces of silver in the temple, and departed, and went and hanged himself" (Matthew 27:5).

The final evidence of conflict that I will cite from the Bible involves the betrayal and eventual crucifixion of Christ. After Christ was betrayed by Judas, He was handed over to Pontius Pilate and the people demanded that He be crucified. The conflict here involved the manner in which Jesus went about teaching the word of God. The people didn't agree with the way in which the word of God was being taught, so they decided that the way to get rid of the opposition was to kill Him. This can be found in St. Luke 23:18.

In a very suggestive and subjective manner, Augsburger endeavors to analyze the ministry of Jesus from the perspective of conflict management and suggests styles evidenced in Jesus' life. For example, the 1,1 or loose-leaf style is suggested when Jesus chose to withdraw from the hostile crowd at Nazareth (Luke 4:16-30), and when He avoided any further discourse with the Pharisees. A 9,1 approach or win-lose strategy is seen where Jesus physically drove the money changers out of the temple (Mark 11:15-19); and where He verbally attacked the hypocrisy of the Pharisees (Matthew 4:23). The 1,9 or yield-lose method is depicted by the suggestion of Jesus that one turn the other cheek, and by His own submission to the cup of agony and death. A compromising or 5,5 position is pictured as Jesus advocates rendering just dues equally to God and to Caesar (Mark 12:13-17), and as He both critiques and concedes to His mother's request at the wedding feast (John 2:1-11). The optimal 9,9 way of confrontation or win-win orientation is demonstrated by the high regard Jesus gave to relationships as well as results in cases like Nicodemus (John 3:1-15) and the woman at the well. However, Augsburger's application is for illustration only and not to critique Jesus.

The one style most often associated with Christ and Christian teaching has traditionally been the 1,9 yield-lose. This style is also referred to as pacifism or turning the other cheek. Bach considers the approach to be a "religious dance," i.e., a process whereby anger is suppressed in a roundabout and unhealthy manner.[1] For him, it is a stance that can deny legitimate anger and circumvent creative conflict. But is that what Jesus intended when He said to turn the other cheek? Did He really advocate pacifism over and against confrontation?

The example to turn the other cheek is more understandable if two factors are kept in mind according to Broadus.[2] First the teaching of Jesus in this passage is not normative but corrective. He is attempting to overcome a destructive attitude of revenge and retaliation common in that day among the Jews. Second, extreme cases have been selected here by Jesus in order to emphasize the underlying principle more vividly. Therefore, in an attempt to develop a more positive spirit, it would be better to turn the other cheek than to be consumed with hate and to retaliate. With reference to the same example, Arndt draws some of the following conclusions: (1) it is not to be taken literally; (2) it is an illustration not an absolute rule; (3) it is intended to counter hate and hostility; and (4) it is to inculcate a positive and loving response.[3] To summarize Jesus is not advocating pacifism or turning the other cheek as best or only way to handle conflict. The basic principle in turning the other cheek is to make a positive and loving response

---

[1]Bach and Goldberg. *Creative Aggression*, p. 165-167.

[2]John J. Broadus Commentary on the Gospel of Matthew, Philadelphia: The American Baptist Publication Society, 1886), p.119.

[3]William F. Arndt, *The Gospel According to St. Luke* (St. Louis, Missouri: Concordia Publishing House, 1956), p. 193-94.

76

instead of a negative and hostile one; i.e. to act constructively instead of destructively in the face of conflict.

The other passage for exegesis is Luke 17:3-4, on dealing with personal offenses which reads as follows:

> Take heed to yourself; if your brother sins, rebuke him, and if he repents, forgive him; and if he sins against you seven times in the day, and turns to you seven times and says 'I repent,' you must forgive him.

This passage is part of Jesus' overall teaching on the journey to Jerusalem, and is included in a specific section of offenses and forgiveness. Matthew 18:15-22 is a parallel passage but much more elaborate. Matthew has apparently taken the initial saying of Jesus as given by Luke (Q) and expanded it into a set of rules for church discipline. It is the most distinctly ecclesiastical passage in Matthew and suggests an organized church structure beyond the scope of Jesus' teaching.[1] Luke's accounting on the other hand presupposes that all such offenses can be decided in a spirit of brotherhood by the parties involved without any thought of appeal to a larger church body. Thus Matthew 18:15-22 appears to be a later development and to be attributed to Matthew's own tradition (M) while Luke 17:3-4 seems to be the more primitive account and to be equated to the original saying of Jesus (Q).[2]

---

[1]Beare, *The Records of Jesus*, p.139.

[2]Manson, *The Sayings of Jesus*, p.139.

A FORMULA FOR GROWTH IN CONFLICT

The verse to be considered exegetically is Ephesians 4:15, which is treated by Clinebell[1] and Augsburger[2] as a growth formula for the management of interpersonal conflict. The verse reads thus: "Rather, speaking the truth in love, we are to grow up in every way into Him who is the Head, into Christ." Unity in Christ is the overall theological emphasis of the book. The verse under discussion is contained in the practical section, Ephesians 4-6, and is part of the first exhortation to promote the unity of the church, Ephesians 4:1-16.

The "truth" contemplated is the truth of the Gospel as indicated in verse 14. This truth is to be confessed or professed "in love." It should be noted that the phrase "in love" does not go with the verb "grow up." First of all, the normal word order joins the phrase to the preceding participle, which would stand in isolation without this modifying phrase; and second, the idea to grow in love is expressed in the very next verse which would be a needless repetition.[3]

To speak the truth in love means here to confront false teaching with sound doctrine in an attitude of genuine care and concern for others. As Marcus Barth puts it, "Orthodox teaching can not and

---

[1] Clinebell, *Growth Counseling for Marriage* Enrichment, p. 11.

[2] Augsburger, *The Love Fight*, p.3.

[3] Charles Hodge, *A Commentary on the Epistle to the Ephesians* (Grand Rapids: Wm. B. Erdmans Publishing Company, 1954), p. 239-40.

must not be promoted at the expense of love."[1] Applied in general, in principle would be to confront others with the truth in a spirit of mutual love.

The result of speaking the truth in love is that "we shall grow up." Since the action of the verb is intransitive, the accusative, "all things," is not translated objectively but adverbially. The meaning is therefore not to "grow all things," but to "grow in everything," e.g., totally or fully. This growth is further defined as being "into Him who is the head, into Christ." Other possible translations of "into Him" are "unto Him" and "toward Him." The idea is "growth toward" a goal with Christ as the Head.[2] This compares to the goal of "mature manhood" and "the measure of the stature of the fullness of Christ" in verse 13. Beare sums it up quite well by saying:

> The way of truth and love, which leads to spiritual maturity, brings us more and more deeply into the unity of a common life with Christ as we are progressively assimilated in our whole being to the nature of our Lord.

---

[1] Barth, *Ephesians* 4-6, p . 444.

[2] Beare, *Ephesians*: Introduction of Exegesis, p. 694.

Based on the principle that speaking the truth in love leads to growth, Clinebell has devised the following formula:

CARING + CONFRONTATION = GROWTH[1]

The term "CARING" has reference to love, while "CONFRONTATION" pertains to speaking the truth. For growth in personal relationships, it takes both affirming love and honest openness. Otherwise, loving affirmed with our honest confrontation is experienced as incomplete acceptance. Consequently, honest confrontation without loving affirmation is experienced as censure or rejection. Augsburger has restated the same formula from a theological perspective: "Judgment and grace lead to salvation."[2] God's grace is His undeserved love which reaches out to accept and affirm. This leads to salvation or greater spiritual wholeness. Again, it takes both for judgment alone would be utter condemnation, and grace alone would be cheap grace. In the case of marriage as in any close fellowship, the general principle would also be the same: Truth + Love = Growth. That means communication that is stated both honestly and lovingly by each spouse.

Ephesians 4:25 thus expresses a unique growth formula. Basically, it has reference to spiritual unity and maturity in Christ to be attained by speaking the truth of the Gospel in a spirit of mutual love whenever doctrinal problems arise within the

---

[1]Clinebell, *Growth Counseling for Marriage Enrichment*, p. 11.

[2]Augsburger, *The Love Fight*, p. 13.

80

fellowship of believers. Applied generally, the principle would be that healthy growth in close personal relationships is facilitated whenever conflict occurs by confronting others with the truth in a positive and loving manner. With regard to marital conflict, honest confrontation coupled with loving affirmation can result in constructive resolution and interpersonal growth.

SUMMARY

In chapter two, biblical concepts from the Old and New Testament were examined with regard to marriage and conflict. An overview of marriage in the Bible was presented first which indicates that the marital relationship is intended to be monogamous in form, mutual in nature, unitive in purpose, and to endure for life in the face of crisis or conflict. In an exegesis of the Genesis stories to the priestly account in Genesis 1:27, the primal couple are found to be created as equal, while in the Yahwist narrative of Genesis 1:18-24, the essential character of their union is described as a mutual one. However, as explained in the Fall in Genesis, the primal couple rebel against God and their disobedience results in sin and marital disharmony.

A brief theology of conflict was also presented wherein conflict is viewed as both an integral and an inevitable part of life, often being expedient as well as necessary. However, it is to be channeled toward a constructive outcome, with real peace being accomplished and well-being attained through conflict resolution. The biblical understanding of anger was still another matter that was examined. Although most references to anger in the Bible were found to be negative due to the destructive consequences associated with the emotion, a limited or appropriate anger was still considered to be justifiable for God and humankind. An exegesis of Ephesians 4:26-27 further revealed that anger which was aroused justly should be dealt with constructively on a day-to-day basis rather than held over and allowed to become sinful or destructive hostility.

Methods of handling conflict were considered next, and it was observed how Augsburger applied the five basic styles of conflict management to the life of Jesus. An exegetical study of Luke 6:27-31 and (Matthew 5:38-42) demonstrated that Jesus does not advocate pacifism or turning the other cheek as *the* Christian method of handling conflict. As shown by an exegesis of Luke 17:3-4 (Matthew 18:15-22), Jesus instead encouraged a 9,9 style of one-to-one confrontation within the context of a close or intimate relationship. The last item to be considered was a speech which can be stated thus: Truth + Love = Growth. The general principle is that healthy growth in close personal relationships is facilitated whenever conflict occurs by confronting others with the truth in a positive and loving manner.

As this chapter indicates, there is a very significant correlation between the concepts drawn from the Bible and those taken from the behavioral sciences with regard to the management of marital conflict. In fact, the only important difference in this project is that pertaining to the venting or free expression of anger and hostility. More often than not, conflict was generally considered to be dysfunctional. But I believe that under certain conditions conflict can be positively functional. Conflict often helps to clear the air and facilitate the maintenance of relationships during periods of stress. It may also serve to remove dissociating elements in a relationship and to reestablish unity. Conflict can further act as a stimulus for the formation of new rules, norms and behavior by those involved. The degree of conflict may likewise be a positive index to the stability of the relationship in that there is enough security and strength to deal with differences. Essentially, it is conflict over issues that do not contradict the basic assumptions upon which the relationship is based that tends to be productive. On that matter, the Bible is very clear that conflict is detrimental and should be restricted. Since conflict within the church is mostly associated with potential violence, there is a tendency for a quick resolve. This tendency is not always true to the biblical account of conflict, e.g., Paul and Mark encountered conflict while on a missionary journey that ended in their separation and prevented them from journeying together again. Thus the data presented from both science and Scripture form a unified framework for the conceptual basis of this project on marriage enrichment for newly married couples.

CHAPTER V

LEARNING TO LOVE AGAIN

Persons who are contemplating the initiation of a new family unit are dedicated to the concept of the "ideal" relationship. They are in love. In spite of the problems they may have observed within their parents' marriages or even in those of their peers, they are convinced that their relationship is unique and therefore immune to boredom and destructive conflict. Many married couples are able to achieve a special relationship – not because they are free from cultural stressors but because they recognize and work with their strengths and weaknesses. After many years of marriage these couples will say that they are more in love than when they left for their honeymoon.

A successful union does not just happen because the individuals wish for it. A successful, functioning relationship requires a realistic appraisal of each situation. It requires sacrifice, forgiveness, commitment and planning. In short, a good relationship is earned – it is worked for – and is not automatic because two people love each other.

A good union begins long before a couple pledges their marriage vows. It starts with two people who have learned to know themselves, their goals, and value systems. These factors become guidelines during the courtship as they look for someone with compatible goals, values, and approaches to the exigencies of life. Gradually, through an honest and open sharing, two persons develop a mutual respect that cherishes the uniqueness of each one and yet binds them together in their understanding of life and hopes for marriage and family.

CHOOSING A PARTNER

The method of choosing a life partner varies widely among cultures, and has changed radically in western cultures during the past two generations. Today, marriage is preceded by a person of increasingly intense social pairing, which offers the opportunity to gradually narrow the potential options for choice of a permanent partner.

Most individuals date several persons prior to marriage, with no commitment beyond the actual agreement for the date itself. Many people date for the fun of it. In some cultures, it is considered unusual and immoral to date without a marriage commitment or without at least an interest in exploring that option.

Dating offers the opportunity to learn interpersonal skills. Individuals get to know how others think and react to events. They learn that there are differences in emotional responses and expressions. They teach each other how to adjust their behavior to meet the other's needs and how to behave in a new situation. They learn negotiation, the "give and take," which is so essential in a relationship. Most importantly, dating helps the individual to learn about him or herself by clarifying one's value system as it is applied to various situations. Dating lays the groundwork for courtship by helping one to identify what type of person is most compatible with one's personality. Most people are socialized to value certain traits, and they tend to marry someone who exhibits similar characteristics and values. When a couple shares a similar background, they have organized their stocks of experience in a similar fashion. A factor that facilitates communication and reduces conflict of values. The choice of a mate naturally begins with who is available. The individuals' contact group tends to bring together persons of similar class, interest, education and goals.

Eventually, a couple decides that they are in love. Love is usually the only socially acceptable reason for marriage in western culture. The religious institutions of the culture teach that love nurtures marital happiness and family solidarity and, therefore, love must prevail in the family relationship. Immature persons view the experience from the standpoint of "being loved" rather than "sharing love" or "giving love." Consequently, these individuals may fail to learn how to love. They assume that it is easy to love but difficult to find the right person to love. Once they fall in love, they assume it is permanent and fail to expend the effort required to stay in love.

Although it is recognized that love makes a positive contribution to our lives, love is an elusive concept because of its highly personal quality. Infatuation, puppy love, and crushes can elicit many of the same physical responses that are interpreted by the individual as true love. True love is variously defined as a deep and tender feeling of affection or devotion; an intense emotional attachment between two people. A crush is a one-sided love that is usually based on an idealized image of another. Puppy love may be quite genuine, but still immature as yet because of the developmental level and experiential background of the two people involved. Infatuation is a self-centered form of love that grows out of a need to belong to someone.

The idea of love at first sight is a myth. True love is a gradually emerging emotion that is not possible until the uniqueness of the individual is recognized. Infatuation tends to ignore reality and to idealize the loved one, while focusing on physical characteristics — limited experiences and minimal emotional intimacy. The individual often has a blind sense of security or jealousy and refuses to look at the relationship or the other person more deeply for the fear of losing the idealized image. The person is actually in love with love; and is more concerned about self-enhancement and pleasure than about the welfare of the other or the long-range implications of the relationship.

Love may begin with infatuation, but real love arises from the appraisal of the total person. The deeper one knows the other, the more intense and committed the love and the relationship become. Real love also idealizes the loved one, but the image can be checked against reality without a sense of loss because real love can allow the partner to be wholly himself or herself without feeling a need to make the person fit into one's image or value system. Eric Fromm shares that the paradox of mature love is that two persons become one, while remaining separate.

Physical attraction is important, especially in the beginning, but it plays a relatively minor role in an evolving relationship where personality attraction assures a significant role. Feelings of trust and a sense of security are fostered in a mutually affirming relationship, where each looks for ways to enhance the functioning of the other and to strengthen the relationship. Fromm postulates that true love is one that must be learned. We learn to love a specific person as we get to know his or her strengths and weaknesses. We accept and love the total person. Marriage is a reality that is constantly emerging; a relationship which is constructed by the unique interaction of the partners. A healthy relationship begins with two people with strong personal identities. This comfort with one's self is discreetly shared with family and close associates. There is no need to continue to play a role in intimate interactions. As one shares inner values, opinions, hurts, and ecstasies, mutual respect and appreciation are developed.

Love springs from a desire to share one's self and to enhance the other, rather than from a need to fulfill one's self in another. It is in the context of two people with healthy identities that true intimacy evolves into a rich, lasting marriage that fosters the continued growth of each member.

God's love finds its fullest manifestation in Christ's provision for the salvation of sinful people. The apostle Paul says this in Romans 5:1-5, "If you want a visible definition of love, look at what God did for us in Christ." If you really want to understand love, don't listen to "rap" music. Don't listen to people who throw the term "love" around. If you want to get to the depths of what it means to love and be loved, look to the death of Christ because there God's love came to mankind.

With the Cross of Christ as the ultimate definition of God's love, I want to suggest six elements of true love. If you want to know whether you love God, this will tell you. If you want to know whether you love your mate or anyone else, this will tell you. What God did for us in Christ is the starting and ending point of any definition of love. Love must have these six criteria to be genuine.

True love is:

Visibly Expressed

True love does not just say "I love you" but true love is always visibly expressed. God expressed His love in creation. You can look around you and see proof of God's love, but creation is not the greatest demonstration of God's love. God showed His love most clearly in redemption, Jesus Christ hanging on the Cross for all to see. That's the message of Romans 5:8.

Invisible love is no love at all. If people have to read your mind to know you love them, they will never really know they've been loved. True love always can be pointed to; it's an activity which constantly says "I love you." So the question is, how are you demonstrating your love? God so loved that God gave Hiss son, John 3:16. No demonstration of your love can ever be too costly compared to this demonstration.

Always Sacrificial

True love is always willing to pay a price for the benefit of another. John 3:16 reminds us of how deeply sacrificial God's love is. If you want to measure your love for someone, or his or her love. If a man will not sacrifice anything for the woman he claims to love and wishes to marry, she's not the one. True love is sacrificial.

A tremendous price tag is attached to true love. Just look at the price paid by Jesus Christ. Too many people, though, do not understand or appreciate the price of Calvary. That is why God doesn't get much look back from us. Some people even dare to question whether God loves them. But God says love at the price I paid for you. Look at the fact that when you were hopeless, when you were sinful, when salvation was totally out of your reach, I gave my son for you — that is how much I love you. It is safe to say no one else has ever loved you like that. Probably no one has ever stepped forward to put his or her life on the line so that you might live. No one else has volunteered to take all the strokes of your punishment — especially someone you had mistreated or hurt. We are not into suffering that much. Loving in God's way involves sacrifice. It costs you something to love. True love is never free. When it comes to love, you must always count the cost and ask "do I want the tab?"

91

Always Beneficial

True love always seeks to benefit the one loved. It does not ask first "what am I going to get out of this?" but "what am I going to put into this so that the one I love can get something out of it?" Godly love does not seek its own but rather that which is beneficial to another. The person who doesn't deserve love actually needs love more, not less. If you know someone unworthy of love, that's great! You now have a chance to emulate Christ because the essence of Christ's love is unconditional. If your love truly reflects God's love, it is not predicated on the other person's earning it, but on your decision to give it. In Deuteronomy 7:7-8, God tells Israel, "I did not set My love on you nor choose you because you were more numerous than any other people, I have loved you and kept the oath which I swore to your forefathers." God decided to love Israel.

True love does not have to be earned. If it did, God would have stopped loving us a long time ago.

Judicial

The fact that God's love is unconditional doesn't make it weak and accepting of everything. Here we find a major difference between divine love and what so often passes for love among people. Of course, being sinful creatures we think selfishly and want to know "what's in it for me?" The fact is, there is something for us in true love. Love does not cancel out your own interests, but your benefit is not the focus. Instead, you want to make sure you accomplish a beneficial goal for someone else. Romans 5:9 reveals a tremendous benefit that Christ purchased for us when

Christ demonstrated God's love. Christ died for us to save us from "the wrath of God." He had our interests in mind.

Unconditional

God's love is not tied to the worth of the person being loved. If that were the case, none of us would have been saved because Romans 5:8 tells us what our "worth" was before God: "we were yet sinners."

Jesus did not wait until we got better to die for us. He died when we were in our most unlovely state. Remember that silly line from the famous sixties' movie, A Love Story? "Love means never having to say you're sorry." Sorry, but that's poor love and even worse theology. God's love always makes judgment calls. Put it this way: "love does not rejoice in unrighteousness, but rejoices in the truth." (I Corinthians 13:6) Love hates what is wrong and embraces what is right.

Some people believe that if you love them, you have to accept anything they want or do. No — love always makes judgment calls. God is very concerned about right and wrong. Love does not tolerate wrong, so the loving thing to do is to correct.

In fact, God says "If I don't correct you, it's because you are not My child." So, if you go year after year rebelling against God and never get corrected, your problem isn't that God hasn't gotten to you yet. Your problem is you are not saved. If you are the devil's child, God may not mess with you. But He says, you are My child, I'm going to wear your backside out because I love you.

Emotional

Don't let anyone tell you that love does not feel. True love always feels. Emotion by itself doesn't equal love, but you cannot have true love without feeling. God feels God's love. The Bible says God delights in the work of His hands. God takes joy in His love for us. Paul says that love "rejoices" when the truth wins out (I Corinthians 13:6). Sometimes we emphasize the caring aspect of agape love so much we negate the emotion of it.

In fact, Paul told the Philippians (chapter 1:8) that he longed for them with "the affection of Christ Jesus." Any definition of love is incomplete that does not include joy and deep feeling. It does not mean you feel good all the time, but it means that your love is marked by an overriding principle of joy.

The Bible reveals that for the joy set before Him (Jesus) endured the Cross (Hebrews 12:2). True love always feels. But, please note this crucial distinction: Feeling doesn't necessarily mean you love; but if you truly love you will feel. So God's love is always visible, sacrificial, beneficial, unconditional, judicial, and emotional. We'll spend the rest of our lives trying to live up to that standard

CHAPTER VI

THE DESIGN

AND IMPLEMENTATION

OF THE

MARRIAGE ENRICHMENT PROGRAM

The single motivating factor which led me to attempt this professional project is my vision and commitment to help families stay together and to offer a caring ministry to a congregation with a myriad of problems. Shortly after I assumed pastoral leadership at Bedford Central in Brooklyn, New York, it became clear to me that there was a need for a programmatic pastoral ministry to married couples. By that I mean a viable ministry with innovative activities for couples. There was no effective and meaningful emphasis toward the married at Bedford Central Church. We are living in a world of painful suffering and I wanted to help the laity recognize that they are called to be partners with me in the ministry. Meeting this challenge would present a new image of our church as a caring, resourceful and family church.

The first meeting of the Advisory Committee convened in the church parlor. Some nine persons were personally contacted, who showed a willingness to devote much time and work in listening and understanding the needs of married couples. Five individuals were selected to form this Advisory Committee. This committee was selected based upon their Christian commitment, leadership skills, knowledge of church and community, and willingness and education to the program to married couples. Inclusiveness and balanced representation were taken into consideration. I outlined at this meeting the design, goal, and purpose of the project using the prospectus as a guide. The evening's agenda included a sharing of each member's concerns and what they perceived as the greatest challenge to married couples. There was also emphasis that both the strengths and weaknesses of marriages should be examined. Emerging from the evening's discussion was the fact that the program would be meaningful for ministry of the church. We also addressed briefly, the procedure for recruiting couples. No definite decisions were taken and we tabled these matters for discussion at the following meeting scheduled for two weeks later.

The second meeting addressed the implementation and the schedule of the project. At the beginning of the meeting each advisor shared some concern about some strengths and weaknesses of marriage. A report was then given informing the Committee of a list of possible couples and highlighting their availability and what they would bring to the ministry. It was emphasized that couples should be persons whose marriage occurred at our church.

Following this briefing of the Advisory Committee a personal letter was written and sent to each couple soliciting their cooperation in working with this ministry. The response was satisfying as the couples who participated were from the Pastor's own congregation. A list of twenty couples recently married but married not more than five years were contacted. The length of their marriages ranged from three months to over 2 ½ years. Individual ages ranged from seventeen to thirty-four. In the case of five couples, one spouse each had been previously married and divorced. The Advisory Committee decided that the letter written should include an invitation to these couples to attend an informal dessert hour at the church on Monday, November 5, 1990. It was planned as a get-acquainted time and as an opportunity to explain the Marriage Enrichment Program that was to be scheduled.

The next step was to enlist the participants for the program at the dessert hour. Following this, we addressed the content and personnel for our training seminars. It was decided that I should decide the book to be used and also conduct the first two sessions. I suggested the book *Growth Counseling for Marriage Enrichment* by Howard Clinebell, since the book portrays a balanced picture of human relationships. The meeting continued with a discussion of the schedule of the project and the roles of various persons from the Advisory Committee.

PLANNING THE FORMAT OF THE SESSIONS

The Advisory Committee and I organized the orientation and the training sessions. It was decided that at the first session the main activity was for each couple to make a marriage collage depicting their relationship, personalities, likes, hobbies, home, family, job, etc. Poster board, scissors, glue, markers and plenty of magazines for cut out were provided. The finished collages were then shared with the group. At the close of orientation the scope and schedule of the proposed Marriage Enrichment Program was presented. Couples were invited to sign up that night and take copies of chapters *of Growth Counseling for Marriage Enrichment*. Six couples did sign up which was considered to be the maximum number for the program.

FORMAT OF THE SESSIONS

The Marriage Enrichment Program consisted of six sessions. These sessions were conducted on six Monday evenings. Desserts and beverages were served at the start of each evening to set an informal atmosphere for dialogue and interaction. Prayer was also offered at that time.

Every session included several basic parts but not necessarily in this order. First, was the statement of the topic and the objective of each particular session. Second, was a review and discussion of the reading assignments. Third, was the main presentation of the subject material. Fourth, was the use of audio-visuals to reinforce the presentation of material. Fifth, was conducting group activities and learning exercises. Sixth, was explaining the session handout and related materials.

READING ASSIGNMENTS

The study book chapters assigned for reading were from the book, *Growth Counseling for Marriage Enrichment* by Howard Clinebell. This particular text was selected for several reasons. First, it combined both behavioral concepts and biblical insights on marriage. Second, it had helpful learning exercises at the end of each chapter.

The other reading added was the Bible. These passages were selected to correspond with the Session Topics of the program as well as the chapter subjects in the study book. Scripture references were chosen from both the Old and New Testament. The verses covered such areas as anger, communication, conflict, and the marriage relationship. A copy of the assigned reading as correlated to the format of the Marriage Enrichment Program is contained in *Appendix A*.

DESCRIPTION OF THE SESSIONS

Session 1

The first session. Prayer was offered which was then followed by the title of the first session "Ways to Manage Conflict." The main objective was for every couple to become familiar with the five basic styles of conflict management, thereby cultivating an awareness of the advantages and disadvantages of each method. Each couple involved themselves in utilizing various styles of conflict, from the confrontational to compromise, accommodation to withdrawal.

Next on the agenda was the presentation of the main subject material which was done by way of flip sheets on an easel. This allowed for group participation. Subjects covered were a Definition of Conflict, Constructive and Destructive Types of Conflict, Major Issues in Marital Conflict and Personal Styles of Managing Conflict.

In order to help each person identify his or her own style of handling conflict, the group was instructed to complete the second exercise included in the reading. A close facsimile of the exercise is reproduced in *Appendix B*. Biblical insights relative to handling conflict were drawn from Luke 6:27-31 on turning the other cheek, and from Luke 4:3-4 on affecting a one to one confrontation. In addition to these perspectives, the life of Jesus was employed as a model to exemplify the various styles of conflict management.

As a review, the couples were each asked to choose a different conflict management style and to role play that method of dealing with conflict in a one minute skit of their own creation. The styles dramatized were then criticized by the entire group with respect to the advantages of each method. Before the closing prayer, a brief period of time was allotted for questions and comments from the group pertinent to the area of conflict covered in the sessions.

Session 2

The second session was convened, the topic of discussion was "How to Communicate Better." The specific purpose of the sessions was for each participant to develop both the sensitivity and the ability for better interpersonal communication. Attention was focused on the need to communicate more effectively by the use of group exercises and discussions. The importance of self-disclosure and feedback in communication were given special emphasis throughout the session. Time was also spent looking at the key formation which was the context of ultimate relationships. The key verse for biblical input on communication was Ephesians 4:14 to speak the truth in love and thereby grow to full maturity. Clinebell's (1975) growth formula based on the verse was likewise stated: Caring + Confrontation = Growth.

To summarize the session, an episode was role played in which a husband debated with himself whether or not to level with his wife about a new secretary who could be a source of temptation to him. The idea was to analyze the situation in terms of self-disclosure, possible feedback and growth potential. By way of reinforcement, a handout of the Johari Window Awareness Model was distributed at the end of the session. This was explained by means of the overhead projector with a transparent foil, made from the handout model as shown in *Appendix C*. The session was

101

closed by spouses offering a sentence prayer for their marriage as a form of communication to God.

Session 3

The topic for the third session was "What to Do about Anger." Here the strategy was to get in touch with the source of one's anger and to encourage the constructive rather than the destructive utilization of that anger. The group discussed the roles of frustration and irrational thinking in the formation of anger. A helpful principle that emerged from the group was that one must deal with anger on a day-to-day basis lest an emotional buildup results in an explosive blowup. It was emphasized that anger is constructive if and when the informative input is of greater impact for good than the hurt or hostility sustained. Following this discussion, couples were paired off in sets of two to talk about at least one recent incident of anger. As one couple observed and criticized the process, then vice versa. The idea was to uncover some of the faulty thinking that often takes place during periods of anger. To be identified specifically was my "Must" an illogical demand that had unduly or unnecessarily aroused an emotional response.

As a follow up exercise, two couples were then selected to role play separate conclusions on marital anger. On couple acted out a destructive outcome by displaying hurtful hostility, while the other couple dramatized a constructive outcome by demonstrating the informative impact for an effective change in the situation. The session was finally terminated by sharing some biblical insight from Ephesians 4:26-27 about dealing constructively with justifiable anger on a day-to-day basis. A period of spontaneous prayer from the group was used to close out the session.

Session 4

For the fourth session the subject was "How to Structure Needed Changes." The actual goal was to learn some helpful insights and skills to effect a positive change in both actions and attitudes. To be noted was a phenomenon of well-established patterns of marital fighting that only perpetuate confrontation. The necessity of breaking through such habitual battle tactics was strongly underscored for a better marriage relationship. Couples were encouraged to get unstuck and experience the freedom to change. A procedure for implementing effective changes was introduced and also incorporated in the session as a learning experience.

Biblical insights from the creation and fall of the primal couple were also shared to evidence the need to effect changes. As set forth in Genesis 1:27 and Genesis 2:18-24, the initial relationship of man and woman was revealed to be one of equality and maturity. But as a result of the Fall in Genesis 3, this relationship was found to have deteriorated in a situation of confrontation and a battle between the sexes. However, it was stressed that the marriage relationship of Genesis 3 was not the one God had originally intended, but rather the model as presented in the creation accounts of Genesis 1-2. The question which the group discussed was how to achieve the more positive relationship, and the answer suggested was to structure needed change.

103

The remainder of the session was allotted to the couples' discussing needed changes and learning how to structure for such changes. The session ended by couples praying in pairs for one another regarding the changes contracted.

Session 5

The caption for session 5 was "Why Not Risk Trust?" The principal aim was to stress an orientation of trust and cooperation against mistrust and contention. The group activities were designed to build and attitude of trust and cooperation. Scripture was utilized to illustrate a model of marriage based on mutual love and trust between spouses. An exercise from the chapter on trust behavior was introduced to start the session. A copy of the exercise is included in *Appendix D*. The entire objective of the experience was for each person to identify his or her own behaviors of trust and distrust. Following this discussion a trust fall was enacted. Detailed instructions for this exercise are given in *Appendix D*. Here the purpose was to risk trust and to get in touch with the inner feelings and sensations that accompany trust and/or mistrust.

The biblical passage Ephesians 5:21-33 was examined as the most significant model for marriage in the New Testament. The principle to be emphasized from these verses was that of mutuality. The responsibility of husband and wife was viewed as loving, respecting, and caring for one another. Trust and cooperation in contrast to mistrust and contention were noted as important factors for such a mutual and reciprocal relationship. To experience a sense of trust and cooperation, the group was asked to participate in a trust walk described in *Appendix E.*. Succeeding that activity the leader gathered the group in a circle and offered a personal prayer for each couple.

Session 6

"Where to Place Blame and Guilt" was the title of the final session. The object was to alleviate the need for assessing blame and assuming guilt. Concepts from transactional analysis were presented as a method of illustrating the judgmental aspects of a person's ego states. The leader emphasized the particular phrasing of a statement and the special manner of asking questions so as to minimize judgmental language. Biblical references were cited to show how love keeps no score and seeks to end the need to blame.

The session was initiated by reviewing the chapters in *Growth Counseling for Marriage Enrichment*. This was done to focus on some of the dynamics involved in the so-called "blame game." Recognized was the fallacy of always trying to affix blame, especially in intimate relationships like marriage. Following the discussion, several simple ways of altering a judgmental approach on one's own part were presented. For example, "I - statements" were shown to be preferable over "you - statements." The former demonstrates taking responsibility in the first person, whereas the latter puts responsibility and/or blame on the other person. Another suggestion was to put an end to questions as a form of interrogation as well as incrimination, and instead to make affirmations about one's own feeling and accountability.

Two Scripture references were compared on the matter of dealing with blame and guilt, Genesis 3:8-13 and I Corinthians 12:5-7. In the Genesis passage the primal couple were found to

105

have played the first version of the blame game. The man blamed the woman and the woman blamed the serpent for what went wrong in the garden. They each passed the buck instead of being individually accountable and accepting equal responsibility. In the Corinthians passage, the ideal nature of love was examined, underscored especially was the statement in verse 5 of the New English Bible that "Love Keeps No Score of Wrongs." I Corinthians 13:5 (NEB). The session concluded with couples allowed to deal with at least one incident of blame and/or guilt that could be forgiven and forgotten. The final item was the completion of the project evaluation by everyone present as printed in *Appendix F.*

RECOMMENDATIONS

The group recommended that a marriage support ministry be continued as a program of the church with a monthly meeting on the first Sunday after worship.

The meetings will serve to continue the discussion started and to assist in incorporating other couples who could be aided by this support group. A further recommendation was that steps be taken to inform the entire congregation about this ministry and to inform them of persons to contact before crises arise. This will be done by announcements in the church's bulletin or quarterly newsletter.

It was recommended and someone was appointed to be a resource person to gather materials to help those dating or involved in premarriage counseling to be aware of the various resources from this group.

The above recommendations underline the fact that both the church and community will benefit from this project.

CHAPTER VII

A PLAN FOR ACTION

The final activity of our coming together was to complete the evaluation form of the project. As can be seen on the evaluation report (*Appendix F*) the advisors and couples evaluated the Marriage Enrichment Program on a scale of one to five (1-5) using two variables. In addition, they provided comments, both verbal and written, to expand the meaningfulness of the exercise. The couples and committee provided recommendations concerning this ministry of the church and the community. Following are the inputs of the couples and the Advisory Committee evaluation.

The conclusion we made of this project was objective. There were areas in which the couples needed improvement and some weaknesses which needed to be fortified. However, the overall evaluation by the couples of the project was satisfactory. The majority felt the sessions had started something worthwhile that should be continued. The experience was definitely new for most of the participants; therefore, calling upon them to reorganize their priorities and extend themselves more. There was a collective feeling of accomplishment as they had taken a risk that had empowered them to look more closely and honestly at a vital relationship in their lives.

Many persons commented on the preparation they had to make for each session and how that experience forced constructive communication in their homes. Furthermore, the sessions afforded them the opportunity for acquaintance with new people within the church that they had seen before but had failed to realize how much they had in common. The participants also felt that as a unit they were now in a position to serve the church as resource persons and for others who may desire to become involved in a marriage support group.

The participants felt strongly about the evaluation and the leadership of the project. They were grateful for opportunities, for dialogue, and role-playing that created a comfortable atmosphere for each session. As one person remarked, "We have learned so much from each other, we cannot let each other down." From the oral and written, feedback given orally and written the lives of each couple were deeply impacted by the experience of this project.

Discussion from the couples also detailed changes in styles of communication with others and making definite decisions as to how to view their relationships after the sessions. Couples suggested increasing their compromising and collaborating, and decreasing their avoiding and competing behavior. They felt this was definitely a positive change towards greater assertiveness and cooperation. Several couples indicated that the dominant style did not lead to cooperation and that such a style should be minimized.

The conclusion from the couples was that the experience was definitely positive as they were confronted with an experience that caused them to analyze their relationships in a dynamic and constructive manner. There was one major concern voiced by the couples concerning their ability to deal with conflict. They suggested that the effectiveness of one's marriage is contingent upon developing appropriate ways to handle conflict.

There were also some practical suggestions from the groups. Included in their evaluation was the need for more face to face communication between spouses which occurred in one of the meetings. Others recommended that the program should be longer as they felt it was too short. This would enable more communication to take place, since most of the participants believed this area was the most important key to maintaining a marriage. A concluding consensus from the couples was that the

111

program gave them food for thought, by bringing various issues into the open for growth, understanding and awareness.

EVALUATION BY ADVISORY COMMITTEE

The analysis by the Lay Advisory Committee was intended to discern if the original objectives of the committee were achieved, and the possible impact the project had on the participants. Their conclusions were that the program was of a tremendous help and should be recommended to others. It was observed that responses showed a high rating as far as being helpful. The potential value of the program was recognized as having both theoretical and practical results. The Committee determined that six sessions would only be a start in acquiring new skills in marriage enrichment, with more time needed for further progress. Still the fact remains that the program was judged to be of considerable benefit to both the Lay Advisory Committee and to the couples and should be highly recommended to others.

An assessment was made of the impact of the program to the extent of the awareness of the marriage enrichment on couples. Responses of the Lay Advisory Committee verified that the program did make participants much more aware of the various facts of the marriage relationship and improved their ability to handle them.

In re-evaluating the layout of the sessions, some persons of the Lay Advisory Committee indicated a different outline for future reference. The sessions on conflict, anger and blame should be scheduled later while those on communication, trust and change should be grouped first. The reasoning behind the recommendation was that these issues were immediately uncomfortable and difficult for a couple trying to work from conflict to communication. One Lay Advisory Committee member suggested having more exercises on communication such as that experienced with Clinebell's International Marriage Method. This person indicated a need for more emphasis on interpersonal communication as a key to maintaining a healthy marriage. Members also felt their willingness to be part of the program that had provided personal value in assisting them to look at their own marriages.

Another area of discussion was the value of the biblical material. It was assessed from the responses that the biblical material assisted greatly in relating the scriptural insights to behavioral patterns in human relationships. In accordance with the original intention the biblical material utilized throughout was also deemed to be of substantial worth.

ADVISORY COMMITTEE RECOMMENDATIONS

The Lay Advisory Committee recommends that a marriage support ministry be continued as a program of the church with a monthly meeting on the first Sunday after worship.

The meeting would serve to continue the discussion started and to assist in incorporating other couples who could be aided by this support group. A further recommendation was that steps be taken to inform the entire congregation about this ministry and give the names of persons to be contacted. This will be done by announcements in the church's bulletin or quarterly newsletter.

It was recommended that someone be appointed to be a resource person to gather materials to benefit those contemplating marriage or presently involved in pre-marital counseling to make them aware not only of the group but of other resources available.

In the area of local mission and evangelism, it was recommended that we become intentional about reaching out to families in crisis. This would be achieved through the visitation of troubled families or through knowledge given to the group by the church leader.

Finally, it was recommended that an annual marriage enrichment retreat be planned away from the church. This retreat would allow couples to be rejuvenated and inspired in a non-threatening atmosphere.

The above evaluation and recommendations underscore the fact that there is a need within the church and the community for newly married persons to be supported in a non-threatening environment.

CONCLUSION

The task in the development of this Marriage Enrichment Program was to define strategies whereby the authentic identity of people as individuals made in the image of God could be recaptured. The establishing of authentic self-image is critical when one realizes this area is where most couples suffer, since self-destruction has done its harm already. The question of what can this church do to maximize the potential of the marriage relationship is a pregnant one. The question is a critical one in light of the sobering statistics which substantiate time and again, that the plight of marriages today is in many ways worse than ten years ago.

One of the important contributions of this project for me is that I have come to realize that black theology adds a vital concept to marriage enrichment. Black theology generally is a mixture of the slavery experience, the indigenous religions and the Judeo-Christian experience. Black theology is not an abstract philosophical system. It is an actual practice, a coming together of God's people for the purpose of doing God's will and in so doing functioning as God's community.

What was evident to me in these sessions was that the church retains its vitality against extraordinary odds because it was born as an expression of the extended family. This is particularly true of the black church to which I belong. The black church is an extended family. With this concept in mind, the church has a theology containing the potential to deal with the problems of black people, but also has a worth that begins to let it function as an extended family.

This feeling was awakened in me as couples supported each other and started to rethink their support base, recognizing that there is an interdependence in the human situation. Another truth that emerged from the project was on the notion of ecclesiology. Many of the ways the leaders functioned in the group depicted the doctrine of the priesthood of all believers proclaimed by the candidate. We need to re-emphasize this truth and give to the laity a greater authority and participation in the ministry of the church. The formation of the Lay Advisory Committee recognized the mission and possibility of helping the pastor and church to address a needed ministry in the church. In so doing, they discovered their own sense of calling and a position where their gifts from God were exercised. As this Committee extended their gifts, they realized they were the church through their extension to every family in the name of Christ.

A third truth is that the function of the Lay Advisory Committee is also in keeping with the family paradigm. As with siblings in the family, some people will be shy, some aggressive, some compromising, others encouraging or in need of encouragement. The dynamics of these relationships are important for a well-rounded healthy family. In a family, there is the general sharing, necessary for marital survival. In the same manner the family of God will come to the table at the time of worship to eat together (in church at the Lord's Supper, rejoice together) in birth (baptism), weep together in death, and work together to build a new (church) home, when the old one is no longer sufficient.

A fourth truth that the project indicated was that the church shares several basic qualities with the family. The church is an inclusive community. Although the titular heads of many churches are male, the basic reality is that women share the power in the black church. In most churches they are increasingly the role

116

models for young people The church is also an adoptionist community. Unlike other churches, most black churches have historically been willing to accept into the membership persons who are outside the fold. Once accepted, these persons are treated as full participants in the life of and in the decision-making functions of the church.

A fifth truth that emerged from the project is that all cultures can be greatly enriched by developing an ecclesiology built on the ideal of the black extended family. Indeed, this had been the aim and experience of all those who were involved in the project; to make couples aware of a larger support system beyond their immediate families. The African roots of the black extended family point very clearly to the fact that administration of the well-being of the tribe was not a unilateral responsibility but a mutual responsibility. The base of the tribe's life was the mutuality with which decisions were made. Elders, chiefs, wives, and children all had voices in the decision-making process. The denial of a voice to any member of the family is not an African but a western tradition. Ours was a message of inclusiveness and love for our neighbors, sensitive to the kind of world in which we live. The praxis of black theology is built upon the principles of mutuality of suffering, inclusion, adoption and hope.

The first observation that I would like to make relates to the future of the project with the church. A theology capable of handling the complexities of black life must be holistic. Blacks have tended to avoid private and group counseling because even verbalization of certain psychological feeling-level matters presupposes certain personal and societal a priori understanding in which black culture is not present. Skills development attempts through classroom experiences are often futile unless other matters are also being addressed. Couples who might come to such

117

sessions cannot hear cognitive material at the deepest core of his or her being, if the primary problem being faced is one of physiology, self-esteem or the need to be loved.

For this reason, what was evident in some sessions was the reality that the family and the church functioned as co-sufferers. It seemed that this is the point at which a church program to enrich the family begins. Such a program must begin by realizing the depth of human alienation and lack of self-acceptance before the most immediate problem is faced.

The offshoot of understanding this basic reality is that any effective marriage enrichment program in the church must be both holistic and patient. Such a program must be holistic because the enrichment the couples need to deal with the various situations that arise in marriages are constantly changing in the inner city. Therefore, any church that is attempting to deal with improving the plight of couples must use strategized methods, tapping the best resources available, to be productive in the area of ministry. The greater burden is being placed on the church in the relentless search to satisfy the needs of the many persons in the pews who are hurting in their marriages.

Another factor that emerged from the study was the confirmation of the disintegration of family life and the need to redefine important ingredients of a marriage enrichment program. The development of a program where individuals can experience the wholeness necessary for the ultimate development of a broad-based system of family stability will not come quickly. The church developing this ministry must be sensitive to the needs of the persons that are being worked with, and must develop a number of different kinds of levels of programs, flexible enough to deal with the awesome differences within the church community. What this means is that although all the couples were within five years of marriage, their ability to verbalize relational and emotional matters well enough to communicate with each other, needed more developing. The Marriage Enrichment Program must continually work to keep an equilibrium between the individual needs and that of the other spouse. This project seemed to renew my commitment to the fact that the extended family model holds the potential for maintaining the individual versus societal equilibrium, without simply speaking of a nuclear family as if it were an individual. The extended family structure starts with the sanctity of each individual, understands that each individual has been primarily socialized by mother and father, but then by virtue of family extension sees self, mother, father and spouse as related to others.

The final factor which the project has affirmed is the strategic role that the black church is playing in the lives of families in crisis. The church has been a sanctuary for the dispossessed and those in despair. In a society of disillusionment the church stands as a ray of hope for those in crisis. As the community continues to experience the disintegration of the black family, the church maintains its role as the main source of support, hope and redemption.

As the Lay Advisory Committee interacted with the couples, they were able to help inspire those confronted by difficulties to work through these situations with a sense of hope, through the Scriptures. In each session, the leaders carried a message that God does not condone dominance or injustice in human relationships but mutual submission and tolerance of each other.

Secondly, the Lay Advisory Committee, through their many years of marriages, was able to become helpful as a resource. Because of the knowledge and resourcefulness of one Committee member, persons were made aware of other helpful resources in the community.

Thirdly, the Committee was able to minister to couples by assuring them that there was a place for them in the church. The project confirmed the fact that the church can be an extended family of the "people of God" and it must remain as such. As the extended family, we will have to fulfill our role as a sustainer and motivator of our people.

Finally, upon reflecting on the entire process and implementation of this project on marriage enrichment, the celebration of baptism and communion serves as an excellent model for me for the understanding of marriage. For Blacks, baptism and communion can maximize the place of the church in the life of the family. The purpose of these sacraments is the center and the context of covenantal love. Because the sacraments speak at the level of the symbolic, they have a much greater potential to give a clear message about human relationships.

Galatians 3:27-28 outlines very clearly the New Testament sense of equality.

"For all of you who were baptized into Christ have clothed yourselves with Christ. There is neither Jew nor Greek, there is neither slave nor free man, there is neither male nor female for you are all one in Christ."

From this text, we can see that Paul speaks of baptism as a way to prevent the placing of persons into stereotypical groupings. Baptism is not always understood this way, but in the black tradition this is a vital issue for us. Baptism is in actuality a sacrament of equality. When the equalizing power of baptism is understood, its potential as a vehicle for unifying family and addressing the equality issues is tremendous. Baptism symbolizes the watery death and the resurrection to this new life of equality. It symbolizes the process of all of us, passing through the same water; it symbolizes our giving of ourselves to each other as Christ has given himself to us.

Hierarchical behavior based on pecking orders is not a biblical concept. The Bible is clear that from the beginning God's image was intended to be an image of mutuality. Baptism reiterates the total mutuality of our human existence. What I have learned through this project is that I must take the time during pre-marital or marital counseling to direct couples to the meaning of their baptism as a way of giving depth to the nature of covenantal love. The powerful symbolism of baptism has an equalizing effect that persons once they become aware, recognize that "we are all one in Christ Jesus."

Just as baptism initiates us into a new order, communion acts as the symbol of our continuance in this role. In communion, we pledge continually our remembrance of God's giving of His self to us. We also pledge our continued bond as a community of faith grounded in God. Communion ultimately models equality because it is served in the same way without respect to persons — rich, poor, male, female, young or old. We receive the bread and wine as our statement of being reconciled with God and with each other. Marriage as a human relationship should be seen in the same light, where reconciliation is viewed as a vital aspect of its function. Just as baptism is important to break down the rigid structures of dominance and submission, communion is important as a way of getting people on an eye to eye level in order to share together with God.

Couples in our church will need to find the strength to rise to the occasion of seeing these events of baptism and communion as having direct impact on their marital relationships. Part of the lesson learned from doing this project is that the church must take seriously, the task of educating people concerning their resources available in the Christian tradition to address most human needs.

SOME PERSONAL LEARNING EXPERIENCES

There is no doubt that this project was straining on my person, physically, emotionally and mentally. But part of my experience was learning when to say "no" and to delegate work to be done. At times I wanted to be in control of the session so much that I lost my rational thinking ability to sit back and allow the discussion to take its own formation. There was a rekindling of my commitment to learn to relax more and not have everything go in my predicted path.

A major gain personally was the training of others to assume leadership responsibilities for the project and the ability to implement a project of this kind in our church. The major concern at first and foremost in our minds was would a black church in the city respond to a marriage enrichment program? Would people keep their commitment and come to the sessions? We persevered and I was convinced that there was a need to implement such a program and to have the congregation involved in it.

Through all the discussions before and after the sessions, I am now better able to listen and accept critical analysis of my ministry. I also learned that there is still a lot of respect and value in the pastoral ministry, as people took seriously the suggestions and answers given to their various concerns. I have come to accept that team ministry is more beneficial than the control-oriented ministry and that I can offer quality leadership which people are looking for in this community.

APPENDIX A

Marriage Enrichment Program
Reading Assignment

First Session:
    Topic: Ways to Manage Conflict
    Scripture: Luke 6:27-31

Second Session:
    Topic: How to Communicate Better
    Scripture: Ephesians 4:15

Third Session:
    Topic: What to Do About Anger
    Scripture: Ephesians 4:26-27

Fourth Session:
    Topic: How to Structure Needed Change
    Scripture: Genesis 1:27; Genesis 2:18-24;
    Genesis 3:18-19

Fifth Session:
    Topic: Why Not Risk Trust?
    Scripture: Ephesians 5:21-33

Sixth Session:
    Topic: Where to Place Blame and Guilt
    Scripture: I Corinthians 13:1-13

APPENDIX B

Session 1

Session Topic:
    Ways to Manage Conflict

Specific Objective:
    To become familiar with various methods of handling
    conflict as well as the advantages and disadvantages of each

Reading Assignment:
    Chapter on "Confronting: The Creative Way Through
    Conflict," pp. 2-13
    Luke 6:27-31

Group Activity:
    One minute skits to role play the five styles of conflict
    management

Subject Presentation:
    Definition of Conflict and Conflict Management
    Types of Conflict and Issues in Conflict
    Personal Styles of Managing Conflict

Biblical Insights:
    Turn the Other Cheek
    Luke 6:27-31

APPENDIX C

Session 2

Session Topic:
How to Communicate Better

Specific Objective:
To help develop both the awareness and the ability for better interpersonal communication.

Reading Assignment:
Chapter on "Truthing It: A Simplified Speech Style," pp. 20-35
Proverbs 15:1; 18:23; Matthew 5:37; Ephesians 4:15

Subject Presentation:
Levels of Communication
Clinebell's Growth Formula
(Caring + Confrontation = Growth)

Biblical Insights
Speaking the Truth in Love Handout
Ephesians 4:15
Johari Window Model

Session 3

Session Topic:
 What to Do About Anger

Specific Objective:
 To explore the sessions of anger and to encourage the constructive use of anger

Reading Assignment:
 Chapter on "Owning Anger: Let Both Faces Show," pp. 40-56
 Ephesians 4:26-27

Subject Presentation:
 Examining the Roots of Anger

Biblical Insights:
 Dealing Daily with Anger
 Ephesians 4:26-27

Session 4

Session Topic:
   How to Structure Needed Change

Specific Objective:
   To learn some of the necessary skills to change actions and
   attitudes for the better.

Reading Assignments:
   Chapter on "Getting Unstuck: Experiencing the Freedom to
   Change,"
   pp. 60-75
   Genesis 1:27, Genesis 2:18-24; Genesis 3:8-19

Group Activity:
   Clinebell's International Marriage Method

Subject Presentation:
   Need for rewriting some old conflict scripts
   Clinebell's International Marriage Method

Biblical Insights:
   Creation of Male and Female — Genesis 1.27
   The Way They Were — Genesis 2:18-24
   A Broken Relationship — Genesis 3:8-19

Handouts:
   Clinebell's International Marriage Method

Session 5

Session Topic:
   Why Not Risk Trust?

Specific Objective:
   To stress an orientation of trust and cooperation as over
   against mistrust and contention.

Reading Assignment:
   Chapter on "Giving Trust: A Two-Way Venture of Faith."
   pp. 80-91
   Ephesians 5:21-33

Subject Presentation:
   Orientation of Trust vs. Mistrust

Biblical Insights:
   Mutuality in Marriage
   Ephesians 5:21-33

Session 6

Session Topic:
   Where to Place Blame and Guilt

Specific Objective:
   To alleviate the need for blame and guilt in marriage

Reading Assignment:
   Chapter 6, "Ending Blame: Forget Whose Fault," and
   Chapter 7, "Case Dismissed: Reclaiming the Gavel,"
   pp.96-104 and 108-118.

Subject Presentation:
   Transactional Analysis (Parent-Adult-Child)
   Elimination of Judgmental Statements
   I-Statements vs. You-Statements
   Putting as end to questions

Biblical Insights:
   Passing the Buck; Genesis 3:8-13
   No Score Keeping; I Corinthians 13:5-7

Audio-Visuals:
   (Transparencies for overhead projection)
   Transactional Analysis Diagrams
   Harris' OK Sequence

Handouts:
   Adult-to-Adult Statements from Transactional Analysis
   Program Evaluation Form

ORIENTATION SESSION

Marriage Collage

Purpose: The objective is to provide couples the opportunity to get in touch with their marriage relationship and to introduce themselves to the group by interpreting their collage.

Procedure: Proceed by using the follow instructions to make a collage as an example of your marriage relationship including family, home, job, hobbies, interests, aspirations, etc.

1. Select poster board, scissors, glue, tape, markers and art materials from the supplies available.

2. Cut out of the magazines provided pictures, words, symbols, configurations, etc., that can be used to describe your relationship as husband and wife.

3. Take about 45 minutes to assemble the collage on one of the tables set up for that purpose.

4. Return to the main meeting area after your collage is completed.

5. Interpret the meaning of your collage/relationship to the other couples in the group when indicated by the leader.

Session 4

Clinebell's International Marriage Method
(How to Structure Needed Change)

STEP I: IDENTIFYING AND AFFIRMING THE STRENGTHS OF YOUR RELATIONSHIP

    A.   One spouse begins by completing the sentence, "I appreciate in you . . .," as many times as possible. Tell your mate all the things you really like. Then the other spouse will do the same.

    B.   Now discuss how you each feel about what you have just done.

    C.   Next, write on a card all the things that each can remember that your spouse appreciated in you.

STEP II: IDENTIFYING GROWTH AREAS — UNMET NEEDS / WANTS IN EACH PERSON

    A.   Again, one spouse will go first and this time complete the sentence, "I need from you . . ." as many times as possible. Tell your mate all the things you really want. Then the other spouse will do the same.

    B.   Now discuss how you each feel about what you have just done.

C.   Next, write on the back of your card all the needs expressed by your spouse to you.

D.   Work together and rate your needs as follows. Put an "A" beside those needs which are the same or similar on both your lists. Put a "C" beside those needs on your two lists which conflict or clash. Put a "B" beside the needs that are left, those that do not contradict the others or are simply different.

STEP III: RECONTRACTING FOR CHANGE — DECIDING TO MEET MORE OF YOUR NEEDS

A.   Discuss the "A" needs on your lists and choose one shared need that is important and achievable to both.

B.   After selecting one "A" need as your marriage-growth goal, decide how and when you will accomplish that.

C.   Then together write out a brief description of the need and how you plan to meet it. Congratulations! You have just written a new clause in your marriage covenant.

STEP IV: TAKING ACTION — CHECKING OUT THE PLAN, IMPLEMENTING IT, AND KEEPING TRACK OF PROGRESS.

A.   The final step is to implement your plan. One way to do this is to have another growth-support couple.

Share your plan with them giving each other feedback and encouragement.

B.   Discuss your experience in checking out your plans as well as how you might use a sharing group or support couple for mutual growth.

C.   Keep a record on the back of your written agreement as to your progress (or regress). Some couples do this in a Marriage Growth Diary in which they make entries of significant events, insights and sharing experiences.

POSTSCRIPT: SATISFYING MORE DIFFICULT NEEDS.

Once you have learned how to use the International Marriage Method (IMM) to satisfy several "A" needs, you may be prepared to move on to the "B" needs. You must learn to negotiate a mutual agreement which satisfies one need of each person. Learning to satisfy "C" needs or those which are in conflict is the most difficult. This requires both negotiation and compromise to find a fair midpoint where each spouse feels some degree of satisfaction.

Adapted from Howard J. Clinebell, Jr., *Growth Counseling for Marriage Enrichment* (Philadelphia: Fortress Press, 1975), pp. 10-17.

APPENDIX E

Session 5

Trust Fall Exercise

Purpose: The object is to risk trust and to get in touch with the inner feelings and sensations that accompany trust and/or mistrust.

Procedure: The following steps are suggested as a guide.

1. Choose a partner whom you feel you can trust and who is willing to trust you.

2. Negotiate the conditions of the fall with the help of the group leader.

   a. If the floor is hard, pads, pillows or blankets may be laid down.
   b. If your partner is unable to catch you alone, a backup person may be used.

3. Face away from your partner and close your eyes.

4. Hold your arms away from the sides of your body to make catching you easier.

5. Signal your partner that you are ready and vice versa.

136

6. Rock back on your heels slowly kneeling over without moving your feet or bending your knees.

7. Focus on your own sensations while falling.

8. Discuss your feeling about the fall experience afterward.

9. Repeat the exercise with your partner in the role of falling and your catching this time, etc.

Adapted from George R. Bach and Yvetta M. Bernhard, *Aggression Lab: The Fair Fight Training Manual* (Dubuque, Iowa: Kendall/Hunt Publishing Co., 1971), p. 89.

APPENDIX F

Evaluation of the Marriage Enrichment Program

Name: _____   Date: _____

(Circle the number on each score line that reflects your honest opinion.)

1. How helpful has the Marriage Enrichment Program been to you?
    Score: Of No Help 1 ____ 2 ____ 3 ____ 4 ____ 5 ____ Of Much Help

2. Would you recommend this Marriage Enrichment Program to other couples?
    Score: Not At All 1 ____ 2 ____ 3 ____ 4 ____ 5 ____ Very Much So

3. To what extent has the program affected your awareness of marital conflict?
    Score: No Change 1 ____ 2 ____ 3 ____ 4 ____ 5 ____ More Aware

4. To what extent has the problem helped you handle marital conflict more constructively?
    Score: No Change 1 ____ 2 ____ 3 ____ 4 ____ 5 ____ Quite Well

5. To what extent has the program helped you communicate more effectively with your spouse?
    Score: No Change 1 ____ 2 ____ 3 ____ 4 ____ 5 ____ Much Better

6. To what extent has the program increased your understanding of your spouse?
    Score: No Change 1 ____ 2 ____ 3 ____ 4 ____ 5 ____ Very Much

7. How would you rate each of the sessions using the following 5-point scale? (Check under the appropriate number; omit sessions missed.)
    Score: Of No Help 1 ____ 2 ____ 3 ____ 4 ____ 5 ____ Of Much Help

    Ways to Handle Conflict   ____ ____ ____ ____ ____
    Ways to Communicate   ____ ____ ____ ____ ____
    What to Do About Anger   ____ ____ ____ ____ ____
    How to Structure Change   ____ ____ ____ ____ ____
    Why Not Risk Trust   ____ ____ ____ ____ ____
    Where To Place Blame   ____ ____ ____ ____ ____

139

8. What would you like to have added to the program that was not included?

9. What other comments, suggestions, recommendations do you have regarding the program?

10. Of what personal value was the program to you in dealing with your marriage?